FASHION AND THE ART OF
POCHOIR

April Calahan & Cassidy Zachary

FASHION AND THE ART OF
POCHOIR

The Golden Age of Illustration in Paris

275 illustrations

Thames & Hudson

This book is dedicated to Dr Lourdes Font, whose passion and vast knowledge have inspired an entire generation of fashion historians.

On the cover: Unsigned, *Journal des Dames et des Modes* (Journal of Ladies and Fashions), 1914 ('Evening coat in crushed velvet lined with silver-embroidered silk').

Title page: Edouard Halouze, *Traité d'enluminure d'art au pochoir* (Treatise on the Art of Illumination Using Stencil), *c.* 1925; plate 13.

First published in 2015 in hardcover in the United States of America by Thames & Hudson Inc., 500 Fifth Avenue, New York, New York 10110

thamesandhudsonusa.com

Library of Congress Catalog Card Number 2015932466

ISBN 978-0-500-23939-1

Printed and bound in China by C & C Offset Printing Co. Ltd

INTRODUCTION
page 6

1

THE ART OF DRESS
Les Robes de Paul Poiret racontées par Paul Iribe
The Dresses of Paul Poiret as told by Paul Iribe
page 18

2

POIRET'S NEW KINGDOM
Les Choses de Paul Poiret vues par Georges Lepape
The Things of Paul Poiret as seen by Georges Lepape
page 34

3

QUEEN OF THE RUE DE LA PAIX
L'Eventail et la Fourrure chez Paquin
Fans and Furs from the House of Paquin
page 52

4

MARTIN AND THE MODISTE
La Mode en mil neuf cent douze chez Marcelle Demay
Fashion in 1912 from the House of Marcelle Demay
page 62

5

STYLIZING 'LA FEMME'
Modes et Manières d'Aujourd'hui
Fashions and Manners of Today
page 74

6

OPULENCE RESURRECTED
Journal des Dames et des Modes
Journal of Ladies and Fashions
page 110

7

ART, FASHIONS, FRIVOLITIES
Gazette du Bon Ton
Gazette of Good Taste
page 138

8

THE FOLLIES OF FASHION
Robes et Femmes
Dresses and Women
page 188

9

AT WAR WITH FASHION
Le Goût du Jour
In Style
page 200

10

THE ARTIST OF LUXURY
La Dernière Lettre Persane
The Last Persian Letter
page 218

BIOGRAPHICAL NOTES *page 232*
FURTHER READING *page 237*
ACKNOWLEDGMENTS & PICTURE CREDITS *page 238*
INDEX *page 239*

INTRODUCTION

'Indeed Fashion is the art of bringing before the mind's eye, on the body of a graceful woman all the wealth of our planet — the precious stones of its mines, the wool of its flocks, the skins of its wild beasts, its silks, flax and cotton, the plumage of its birds and pearls from its seas. A handsome and beautifully dressed woman is therefore an epitome of the earth.' Paul Adam, 1915[1]

In the first quarter of the 20th century, a centuries-old hand-stencilling technique known as *pochoir* was re-imagined and innovatively integrated into the world of fashion publishing. The painterly qualities of the technique – achieved by the application of watercolours or built-up layers of gouache paint by hand – appealed to couturiers and publishers alike who were disenchanted with the machine-printed, mass-circulated fashion publications that dominated the period, such as *Vogue* and *Femina*. They employed the labour-intensive – and, in turn, costly – pochoir process in luxury, limited-edition publications intended for an elite clientele. This book celebrates the mastery and extraordinary beauty of pochoir in fashion publications from 1908 to 1925, a brief but prolific Golden Age of fashion illustration.

Collectively, the ten publications featured in this book document a fashion revolution, in terms of both the clothing depicted and the practice of fashion illustration itself. The groundbreaking illustration styles seen in the pages of these albums and magazines were born out of the need to represent the rapid modernization of fashionable dress that occurred in the first two decades of the century. Illuminated with pochoir, these publications presented a fresh alliance of fashion and art, and challenged the long-held notion that fashion illustration was not a viable platform for true artistic expression. The continued use of pochoir throughout the 1910s and 1920s helped to dramatically redefine the visual landscape of the centuries-old fashion plate, an otherwise traditional advertising tool for dressmakers, tailors and purveyors of fabrics and trimmings. Today, one hundred years later, these pochoir works maintain their extraordinary beauty and appeal owing in large part to the remarkable resilience of the technique. The plates appear to have lost none of their original lustre, and the paint gleams on the page as if it is freshly applied. Private collectors and museums the world over treasure these remarkable – and now exceptionally rare – publications as works of art.

But if the adoption of pochoir (the French term for 'stencil') in the realm of fashion was something entirely new, the technique itself had been used in Europe even as early as the Late Stone Age.

uminator imaginum. **Brieffmaler.**

EFfigies varijs diſtinguo coloribus omnes,
Quas habitu pictor ſimpliciore dedit.
Hic me peniculus iuuat officioſus in omni
Parte, meumǵ vagis veſtibus ornat opus.

Cuiǵ ſuum tribuo quem debet habere colorem,
Materijs cultus omnibus addo ſuos.
Vtimur argenti, radiantis & vtimur auri
Munere, cum rerum poſtulat ordo vices.
Omnibus his furi.as pictoribus imprecor omnes,
Qui bene nec pingunt, nec vigilanter agunt.
Pictor.

An image from *Das Ständebuch* (Book of Trades), published in Latin in 16th-century Germany. The authors, Hans Sachs and Hartmann Schopper, highlighted various professions of the time, including that of *Brieffmaler*, the illuminator of images. The image clearly portrays a man in the process of printing with the aid of stencils – his large brush applies the paint to a work in progress, while the finished products lie in a stack before him. A caption accompanied the print:

A Gilder of Books am I
A Brush my daily Bread supplies
I tint all pictures on paper with parchment
With gold, bright colours and dyes.

POCHOIR: HISTORY AND TECHNIQUE

'Nothing is nicer to see than the studio of a colorist. . .On the tables, the pots of paint sparkle like bouquets of flowers, agile hands doing the pochoir with the brush wet with color, sheet after sheet. What a pleasant spectacle!'[2]

Stencils used in cave paintings found in the Franco-Cantabrian region of France date as far back as 40,000 BC. Much later, Charlemagne, king of the Franks (742–814 AD), unable to read or write, employed stencils to sign his name. Stencils were also commonly used to apply colour to playing cards in the 16th century and to decorate furniture and wallpaper in the 19th.[3] None of the various incarnations of stencilling throughout France's long history, however, even hinted at the level of artistry and sophistication that the technique would achieve at the hands of master technicians in the early 20th century.

It was the Japanese who set the precedent for stencilling as an advanced printing medium to be admired, and eventually emulated, by French printmakers. Guilds of

The pochoir studio of the journal *Art, Goût, Beauté*, taken from *Le Livre d'or* (1930). *Art, Goût, Beauté* was printed and hand-coloured in Lyon, France.

skilled artist-craftsmen across Japan were dedicated to the profession, which had been cultivated and refined over hundreds of years. In the 19th century stencilled kimonos, fans, porcelains and lacquered wares were imported en masse to Europe, where they became prized collector's items.[4] In the 1890s French printmakers, perhaps inspired by Japanese prowess in the technique, began to experiment with stencilling in book publishing. André Marty helped to pioneer the process, known as *pochoir* in France, during this period at his Paris studio, Greningaire et Fils.[5] It was there that Jean Saudé, the future innovator and world authority on pochoir, was apprenticed at the beginning of his career.[6]

As equal parts pochoir scholar, innovator and skilled practitioner, Saudé made unparalleled contributions to the artistic renaissance of the technique in the 1910s and 1920s. George Barbier, whose work from the beginning of his career was produced by Saudé, referred to him as 'the master of coloured prints' who raised the technique of pochoir 'to a degree of perfection never achieved before'.[7] At the hands of Saudé, a once simple, primitive method of reproduction became an intricate, finely nuanced undertaking, a process capable of replicating an artist's original work down to the most minute of details with a skill and finesse unachievable by mechanized processes, and in which Saudé took great pride.

Saudé's impressive oeuvre in the genre spanned the graphic – and economic – spectrum, and included everything from inexpensive postcards and catalogues to luxury-edition *livres d'artiste*, murals and even textiles.[8] To this day, Saudé's *Traité d'enluminure d'art au pochoir* (Treatise on the Art of Illumination Using Stencil; 1925) remains unrivalled; it is the single most important and authoritative resource on the pochoir method. In it, Saudé draws on more than thirty years of experience to present the history of the stencilling process, a critical analysis of the current state of the craft, and a discussion of the various methods and techniques involved in its application, complete with detailed pictorial examples. The book itself is an exemplary testament to pochoir, as every single image is produced using the technique. The examples range from single-layer illustrations with a faint, monochrome palette to decidedly more complex applications involving numerous colours, stencils and techniques, as seen on page 9. 'The secret of our art is all in the manipulation of colours', wrote Saudé.[9]

The technique was adopted across the fine and applied arts in the portfolios of artists, architects and interior designers, as well as in numerous books on fine art, poetry, theatre, music and, of course, fashion. After the 1920s, pochoir became the medium of choice for many of the most important artists of the 20th century. Henri Matisse's seminal book *Jazz* was printed using pochoir in 1947, and Pablo Picasso printed over 200 works using the technique throughout his career.

Despite isolated undertakings in England and America, notably by Harold Curwen and Vance Gerry respectively, pochoir remained, fundamentally, a French phenomenon.[10] Daniel Jacomet, who was apprenticed under and eventually succeeded André Marty, ensured the continued success of pochoir into the 1960s through high-profile collaborations with Picasso, Marc Chagall and Joan Miró, among many others.[11]

A FASHION REVOLUTION

The avant-garde couturier and fashion pioneer Paul Poiret was the first to translate the brilliant, illustrative possibilities of pochoir into a luxury album of fashion, *Les Robes de Paul*

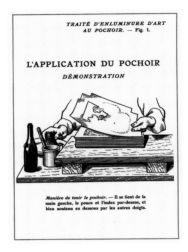   

This page Jean Saudé, *Traité d'enluminure d'art au pochoir* (Treatise on the Art of Illumination Using Stencil), 1925. In the chapter on technique, Saudé provided a detailed pictorial demonstration of the pochoir process, with plates that demonstrate the wide range of hog-bristle brushes that were the principal tools of the *coloriste*. Depending on the type of work, as many as four could be used to apply a single colour. Saudé's book even included a stencil so that the readers could practise the technique themselves.

Opposite, top Jean Saudé, *Traité d'enluminure d'art au pochoir* (Treatise on the Art of Illumination Using Stencil), 1925. The most important part of the pochoir process was the beginning, when the original artwork was scrutinized and broken down into its components. Each colour required a separate stencil, as did any subtleties in texture or tone. It was Saudé's ability to emulate perfectly the nuances of an artist's work, such as the gradation of light in this image, that made him a master of his craft.

Opposite, bottom Here, the illustrator Pierre Brissaud's original ink and watercolour on paper (left) is paired with the pochoir-printed reproduction that appeared in *Gazette du Bon Ton* in 1914 (right). The translation of an artist's original work into pochoir was achieved through a streamlined, step-by-step process. An original work was photographed so that its colours could be analysed. Each individual colour section would then have a photographic proof made; using these proofs, stencils were cut from thin sheets of copper or zinc sheeting by the *découpeur* using a scalpel. These stencils were given to the *coloriste*, who – with meticulous attention to their registration – applied the watercolours or gouache to pages that had typically already been printed with the basic black outlines of the original work. A pochoir print like that seen here could require several dozen stencils, used in a specific sequence to create the desired effect.

Poiret racontées par Paul Iribe. Given as gifts to his distinguished clientele in 1908, the album represents an unprecedented approach to fashion advertising. With the exception of the opening matter, it is completely devoid of text – a dramatic departure from fashion magazines of the day, which typically provided detailed descriptions of the colours, materials and construction of the ensembles illustrated. The novelty of the approach is underscored by the illustrator Paul Iribe's highly stylized renderings of Poiret's gowns. Emboldened by blocks of pochoir colouring, which limited the illusion of a third dimension, Iribe's illustrations read as flat and two-dimensional, more akin to Japanese woodblock prints than to any fashion plate seen previously. But then again, *Les Robes de Paul Poiret* was not the portfolio of a mere fashion designer: 'I am not commercial. Ladies come to me for a gown as they go to a distinguished painter to get their portraits put on canvas', proclaimed Poiret. 'I am an artist, not a dressmaker' – or so he would have his clients believe.[12]

Much of the album's allure had to do with the liberal artistic licence Poiret afforded Iribe in the interpretation of his gowns, which allowed Iribe's work to wander beyond the traditional confines of fashion illustration and into the realm of fine art. This point is reinforced by Poiret's deliberate decision to use pochoir. The saturated colours, achieved by layers of gouache paint meticulously stencilled by hand, create the illusion that each plate is an original work of art. *Les Robes de Paul Poiret*, rendered in this unprecedented manner, effectively blurred the lines between art and advertising and obfuscated what was, ultimately, the commercial impetus

behind the album. Simultaneously, it marked a significant shift in the discourse between art and fashion, and the year of its publication, 1908, remains a turning point in the history of fashion illustration.

Before *Les Robes de Paul Poiret*, there had been nothing particularly modern about the fashion plate. Such illustrations had continued in more or less the same lineage and format since their inception in the 17th century, with a chief objective to convey clearly the latest styles in clothing to a broad audience. Illustrators employed a high level of detail – down to the very placement of buttons and seams – to relay as much information *visually* as possible, while accompanying didactic text informed the reader about the specific colours and materials used in a design and, depending on the publication, often where the goods could be obtained. A typical fashion plate was comprised of a single fashionably dressed figure, or a small group, within a rectangular border. Printed in black and white, these images were then coloured by means of hand-tinting, a large cottage industry with a predominantly female workforce. Similarly, fashion illustration was considered a suitable profession for women, and many women illustrators, notably the renowned trio of Colin sisters, created beautiful renderings with considerable artistic finesse during the 19th century. Even the prettiest compositions, however, did not take their cue or inspiration from contemporary art movements, and over the years such images continued to depict a conventional range of tropes: an afternoon stroll, a visit paid by a friend, playtime with children or a woman at her toilette for an evening ball.

ANDRÉ-MORISSET

EN TENUE DE PARADE

Robe d'hiver pour la promenade

Gazette du Bon Ton. — N° 2   Février 1914. — Pl. 13

Utagawa Kunisada, *Beauty Walking on a Snowy Day*, Japan, 19th century.
Japanese woodblock prints flooded Europe in the 1850s, when trade was
re-established with Japan after a 200-year hiatus. Their popularity quickly
spread, aided by exhibitions that exposed the works to an even wider public.
This growing appreciation culminated in an exhibition at L'École des Beaux-
Arts, Paris, in 1890, at which more than 1,000 examples were displayed.

Paul Iribe, *Les Robes de Paul Poiret racontées par Paul Iribe* (The Dresses of Paul
Poiret as told by Paul Iribe), 1908; plate 8 (detail). The influence of
Japanese woodblock prints, such as the one by Utagawa Kunisada (left)
can be seen in this detail of a plate from *Les Robes de Paul Poiret*. Sharp, crisp
lines and flat planes of colour rule the composition, which gives little
consideration to creating the illusion of a third dimension.

The advent of colour lithography in the 1880s resulted in
a decline in the quality of fashion plates. Hand-tinting was
discarded in favour of less expensive, faster mechanized
processes used in the mass-production of fashion magazines,
and the charming sentiment was replaced by comparatively
static presentations of fashion, replicated quickly and
without the inimitable touch of the human hand.

Les Robes de Paul Poiret not only shattered these static
visual conventions, but did so within the realm of the
artistic avant-garde. Iribe was not a fashion illustrator.
His earlier work had been almost entirely focused on
political satire in a style undeniably inspired by that
of the English artist Aubrey Beardsley. Beardsley, and
subsequently Iribe, drew from a long tradition of artists
who were influenced by Japanese woodblock prints, which
flooded Europe in the 1850s after trade with Japan was
re-established following an interruption of 200 years.
Many Impressionist and Post-Impressionist artists, notably
Mary Cassatt, Henri de Toulouse-Lautrec and Vincent van
Gogh, embraced the stylistic qualities of the prints in an
effort to challenge the principles promoted by France's and
England's official artistic establishments, represented by
the Salon and the Royal Academy respectively. These artists
found inspiration in the prints' portrayal of ordinary

subject matter, as well as their distortion of their subjects,
emphasis on line and bold blocks of colour, and flatness
of perspective. These elements are all found in *Les Robes de
Paul Poiret*.

The revolutionary nature of the illustrations featured
in *Les Robes de Paul Poiret* paralleled that of the fashions they
depicted. The women model high-waisted gowns in a variety
of vivid colours; the clothes cling to their un-corseted frames.
'While studying sculptures of ancient times', wrote Poiret,
'I learned to use one point of support – the shoulders,
where before me it had been the waist. . .Fabrics flowed
from this ideal point like water from a fountain and draped
the body in a way that was entirely natural.'[13] Poiret's designs
provide a striking contrast to the prevailing fashion for the
dramatic S-curve silhouette, which was maintained by rigid
corsetry. He found the style abhorrent: 'The abominable
Gaches-Sarraute [corset] divided its wearer into two distinct
masses. On one side there was the bust and bosom, on the
other, the whole behindward aspect, so that the lady looked
as if she were hauling a trailer.'[14] Or, as the editor of *Vogue*
simply put it: 'Women today are all covered in humps.'[15]
This unnatural 'pouter pigeon' effect was emphasized with
tight-fitting blouses tailored to the narrow waists, and
long, cumbersome bell-shaped skirts supported by layers

of petticoats. The silhouette, while statuesque, represented an entirely unnatural distortion of the body.

This shift in emphasis from waist to shoulders is one of the defining moments in the birth of modern dress, to which we are indebted today. 'It was the age of the corset and I waged war against it', wrote Poiret, who would always maintain that he alone was responsible for freeing women from the corset and 'caus[ing] fashion to evolve toward classical antiquity'.[16] In reality, many other designers, including Madeleine Vionnet, Jeanne Paquin and Lucile (Lady Duff-Gordon), were also experimenting during this period with clothing that revealed the natural contours of the body. Softer, more fluid fabrics and Grecian-inspired drapery accented the corset-free silhouettes, while making clear reference to the fashionable dress of more than a century earlier. Indeed, commentators who attempted to describe the 'sheath' gowns presented by Poiret and his contemporaries turned to France's Directoire period, which directly followed the French Revolution. During this time (1795–99) and into the 1810s, women had similarly discarded their heavily constructed fashions in favour of high-waisted, flowing chemise gowns modelled on Greco-Roman dress.

The modern 'Directoire' fashions were not without their critics – or controversy. In May 1908 three mannequins from an unidentified couture house made international headlines when they were reportedly arrested at Paris's Longchamps racecourse wearing the clinging garments. In reality, the models were not arrested, but the sensationalizing of the event in the press sheds light on public concern over the repercussions of such a significant change in women's dress.[17] Historically, women's clothing has been intimately linked to society's notions of propriety and femininity. The eagerness of many to dismiss the new silhouette as a simple fad was supported by history: the corset, in one form or another, had dominated women's fashion for almost

400 years. Even the French Revolution had not secured its demise. Despite vocal dissent on both sides of the Atlantic about the 'freakish frocks', by the autumn of 1908 women had embraced the high-waisted, body-skimming style; even the most conservative couture houses were forced to adapt to the latest demands of fashion or risk becoming irrelevant.[18] Although the corset would not altogether disappear for some time, it gradually became less and less relevant, its necessity undermined by the demands of World War I, and also by the desires of the modern woman. From 1908 onward, fashion would continue to progress towards modernity with clothing that promoted ease of movement, comfort and practicality over distortions of the body.

This fashion revolution is perhaps not surprising when seen against the backdrop of the dawn of the 20th century, a prolific period of heightened artistic cross-pollination in Paris. The city was a cultural Mecca of experimental expressionism, as various segments of the aesthetic milieu, ranging from architects to dancers, musicians to painters, and interior decorators to publishers, all sought to reinvent their work on the stage of the new century – and the field of fashion design was no exception. As the modern art of Cubism was born from the experiments of Picasso and Georges Braque and modern ballet within the choreography of the Ballets Russes, so too was fashion revolutionized at the hands of visionary couturiers and illustrators.

THE RISE OF POCHOIR BEFORE WORLD WAR I

The Russian impresario Sergei Diaghilev's Ballets Russes took Paris by storm in the summer of 1909. Diaghilev re-imagined ballet within the framework of an extravagant production, in which innovative choreography combined with exciting music, sets and costumes to create a visual symphony unlike anything Parisian audiences had ever seen.

This black-and-white illustration from *Femina* in June 1906 is typical of the fashion plates published in mass-produced magazines of the period.

Les Modes, 1905. Poiret's Directoire-inspired designs contrasted with the then mainstream fashions, which emphasized a tiny waist and a 'pouter pigeon' torso.

Dress by Paquin, *Les Modes*, 1909. Jeanne Paquin, another forward-thinking designer who embraced the Directoire silhouette, raised the waistlines of her

dresses as early as 1905. This dress from 1909 is remarkably similar in shape and spirit to the dress from 1801 (*Journal des Dames et des Modes*, above).

Diaghilev infused the ballet with distinctly Russian elements, but also those associated with a romanticized, exotic 'East', as highlighted in productions such as *Cléopâtre* (1908) and *Schéhérazade* (1910). The productions, notably the fantastic sets and costumes by Léon Bakst, dazzled and enraptured Parisian audiences, and pervaded the zeitgeist of the era. 'A fashion world that had been dominated by corsets, lace, feathers and pastel shades soon found itself in a city that overnight had become a seraglio of vivid colours, harem skirts, beads, fringes and voluptuousness', remembered Cecil Beaton. 'What could be more stark than a revolution that overnight guillotined prettiness and set exoticism upon the throne?'[19]

The most visible purveyor of the Orientalist trend in fashion was Poiret, who was one of the first to translate it into fashionable clothing – and into pochoir. Poiret's Eastern-inspired designs, such as turbans and the controversial *jupes-culottes* (literally 'skirt-trousers'), are found within the pages of his second pochoir album, *Les Choses de Paul Poiret vues par Georges Lepape*, published in 1911. This album was almost identical in format and concept to *Les Robes de Paul Poiret*. The illustrations by Georges Lepape, then an emerging young painter, also borrowed liberally from the stylistic qualities of Japanese woodblock prints. But whereas Iribe had played with the contrast between positive and negative space, Lepape used the possibilities of pochoir to the fullest effect, and each plate was a rich, abundant source of fantastic colour and visual delight – a trait with which Lepape's name would become synonymous. From both Iribe and Lepape, Poiret encouraged unbridled interpretation of his fashion designs. Together, Poiret's two pochoir albums set a high-profile precedent for collaborations between fashion designers and artists that could no longer be ignored. Fashion's leading tastemakers would soon follow Poiret's lead, embracing and embellishing the precedents set by his two pioneering works.

Eight months after the release of *Les Choses de Paul Poiret*, the couturière Jeanne Paquin published an oversized pochoir album illustrating her designs for furs and fans, entitled *L'Eventail et la Fourrure chez Paquin*. The album was followed by the modiste Marcelle Demay's album *La Mode en mil neuf cent douze chez Marcelle Demay* in early 1912, as well as the first edition of the annual *Modes et Manières d'Aujourd'hui*, and the fashion magazines *Journal des Dames et des Modes* and *Gazette du Bon Ton* later that year. The last three publications were especially significant in that they extended Poiret's canons beyond the singular artist portfolio into annual, thrice-monthly and monthly affirmations, respectively, of the art of fashion, while simultaneously expanding the role of the fashion illustrator.

Although Poiret had given Iribe and Lepape total liberty to interpret his designs, they were still *his* designs. In contrast, the fashions featured in *Modes et Manières* were entirely of the artist's fancy, albeit an embodiment of overarching fashion themes from the previous year. Similarly, *Journal des Dames et des Modes* rarely depicted fashion designs by actual *couturiers*,

whereas *Gazette du Bon Ton* offered its readers a combination of both, alternating the artists' original 'designs' with those of the leading couturiers of the day. Confined to the pages of their respective fashion publications, the original ensembles put forward by these illustrators were nothing more than fantasy, albeit a charming suggestion of what fashion *could* be. Georges Lepape argued that the fashion illustrator had a profound influence on contemporary styles: 'He may through his interpretation impose fashion, making it understood and appreciated by the medium of his Art and personality; or, by creating and inventing, he can force fashion to follow in the furrow ploughed by his own imagination.'[20] It was an argument supported by *Vogue*'s editor-in-chief, Edna Woolman Chase: 'It was hoped the *haute couture* would copy them', she wrote of the artists of *Gazette du Bon Ton*, 'more than once the couture did.'[21] Within the pages of these three publications, the line between the fashion designer and the fashion illustrator, two once mutually exclusive roles, became blurred.

The fact that the core contributing illustrators to *Gazette du Bon Ton* were all finely trained artists – and friends – also did not escape the notice of Chase. 'These young men of

SCENE FROM "SCHÉHÉRAZADE"

Opposite Paul Poiret, 'Sorbet' evening ensemble, 1913. In 1913 Paul Poiret created costumes for Jacques Richepin's stage production *Le Minaret*, which featured harem trousers (Turkish trousers) paired with short, flared tunics that were supported with hoops at their hems. This silhouette, which became known as 'Le Minaret', made an appearance in Poiret's fashion collections later that year. This silk evening ensemble was a popular adaptation of the minaret silhouette, instead seen here with a wrapped skirt that gives the illusion of Turkish trousers. This ensemble was depicted by Georges Lepape in the *Gazette du Bon Ton*'s eleventh issue of 1913, in another colourway (see page 159).

Left 'Scene from Schéhérazade', 1916. The costumes seen here for the Ballets Russes production of *Schéhérazade* were the creation of Léon Bakst. As with the costumes he produced for the troupe's earlier production of *Cléopâtre* (1908), Bakst drew inspiration from Eastern dress to create ensembles that were modernist amalgamations of Egyptian, Persian and Ottoman styles.

birth and Beaux Arts training have wrought in the affairs of fashion…a revolution which is sweeping the civilized world', she wrote. 'They bring to their work a knowledge which has made fashion the art of the day instead of art being the fashion.'[22] While not specifically crediting Poiret, Chase acknowledged that until recently, for an artist to dabble in fashion illustration 'would have been considered a profanation of his talent'.[23] Poiret's two albums had validated fashion as an accepted artistic outlet for fine and classically trained artists seeking alternative sources of income, and subsequently paved the way for a new generation of fashion illustrators. The distinctive illustrative styles of Barbier, Lepape, Charles Martin, André Édouard Marty, Bernard Boutet de Monvel and Pierre Brissaud in particular, the group at the heart of *Gazette du Bon Ton*, epitomized the new ideals in the interpretation of fashion that would become synonymous with luxury fashion publications in the ensuing decade.

Prohibitively expensive to all but a select few, these fashion albums and magazines collectively served to underscore the lavish, decadent lifestyles of a wealthy elite in the years before World War I, a point of jest in not one but two pochoir albums dedicated to the follies of fashion. *Robes et Femmes* (1913) and *Le Vrai et le faux chic* (1914) both provide a satirical – albeit beautiful – commentary on the acquiescent, careless attitudes of the few who could afford to follow fashion's every whim. Fashion was just one aspect of the *bon vivant*'s lifestyle of luxury and unrestrained decadence that defined the period often referred to as the Belle Époque. Alas, the 'Beautiful Age' was not to last.

FASHION DURING THE WAR

'All through that last brilliant pre-War summer Paris amused herself, spent recklessly, gave wonderful fêtes, laughed, danced and made love as though she had not a care in the world. And nobody saw the war clouds gathering until they burst with shattering suddenness', remembered the couturière Lucile. 'In one week, Paris was a changed city.'[24]

Essentially, the assassination of Archduke Franz Ferdinand, heir presumptive to the Austro-Hungarian throne, precipitated the beginning of World War I, but in reality events were much more complicated. The war was the result of long-standing colonial and racial tension between Austria-Hungary and Russia. When the two countries went to war in July 1914, they brought with them their allies: the 'Triple Alliance' of Austria-Hungary, Germany and Italy against the 'Triple Entente' of Russia, France and Great Britain (and later the United States of America).[25]

World War I was the first modern war. The Industrial Revolution of the 19th century had bred rapid technological advances in weaponry, communications and transportation that redefined warfare on an epic and devastating new scale. A survey in 1920 of the cost of the war calculated that a total of 12,996,571 soldiers lost their lives, an overwhelming number estimated to have been equalled by civilian deaths.[26] On top of the devastation of the war, a flu pandemic swept through Europe in 1918 and 1919, and between ten and twenty-seven million people lost their lives.[27]

There was no place for pochoir fashion magazines in the harsh reality of war, just as there was no place for the lavish public consumption of luxury or entertainment of any kind.[28] *Gazette du Bon Ton* and *Journal des Dames et des Modes* suspended publication as soon as war broke out, while French couturiers were left questioning the fate of their businesses – and their own lives. Some couture houses shut their doors as their male designers and employees joined the millions of men across France subject to compulsory military service. In early August 1914 the American department-store magnate John Wanamaker visited Poiret's atelier, where he found the designer in uniform surrounded by his weeping, faithful staff: 'An artist is nothing when a soldier is wanted', Poiret told him. 'France needs men today, not artists.'[29] Indeed, the head designers at many of Paris's most prestigious couture houses, including Worth, Premet and Martial et Armand, were all called to service.

AT THE DRESSMAKER'S
Dress from Lanvin

Far left Les Modes, 1914. A rapid shift in silhouette occurred between 1914 and 1916. The narrow hobble skirt seen here, popular during the years before World War I, was replaced by a shorter, flared skirt.

Left The 1915 Mode as Shown by Paris, 1915. Threatened by America's fashion-design potential, Parisian couturiers sent their designs to be featured in not one but two separate exhibitions in 1915, one on each of America's coasts. This photograph captures two of the models sent by Jeanne Lanvin to the Panama Pacific International Exposition in San Francisco. Later that year, couturiers would send their work to be featured in *Vogue*'s Fashion Fête in New York City.

Parisian couture, as the recognized world leader in fashion, was the driving force of France's clothing and textile trades, which combined formed the second largest industry in the country, employing 34 per cent of the nation's labour force.[30] Couture kept hundreds of thousands of people employed across France in a wide spectrum of jobs. From the ateliers of the couture houses themselves to their numerous suppliers in textiles, dyes, embroidery and lace, to the dozens of offshoot industries, such as fur, millinery and footwear – all depended on couture as a compass for taste and style. That is not to mention couture's foreign clientele: America's multimillion-dollar clothing industry, whether ready to wear or made to order, revolved around demand for Parisian, not American, design. 'Yes, it is hard to write about godet skirts instead of uniforms; of French fashions instead of French humanity', wrote the *New York Times* shortly after the beginning of the war, 'but the world of trade must go on if those millions left behind are to eat.'[31] It was an economic imperative for Parisian couture to carry on sales and production without interruption.

The question was how. War broke out on the eve of the autumn fashion shows, and with some couture houses closed indefinitely and others on limited operations, the fate of the *grandes maisons* was uncertain. The couture houses that did remain open – many of them run by women, including Callot Sœurs, Chéruit, Jenny, Jeanne Lanvin and Paquin – were left to define the new gravitas in fashionable dress.[32] Collectively, the houses of the Chambre syndicale de la couture parisienne, the governing association of French couturiers, agreed not only to move forward with the

autumn fashion shows as planned, but also to unite in promoting a new style that had just begun to emerge before the war.[33] In August 1914 a new silhouette featuring a shorter, flared skirt supported by crinolines was seen almost across the board in Paris collections. The antithesis of the ultra-narrow, floor-length hobble skirt, this skirt moved away from the body as it descended from the high natural waist, and terminated with a generous hem circumference several inches above the ankles. 'With her back against the wall of Paris. . .fashion defends her right to life, liberty, and the pursuit of woman', wrote *Vogue* on the new collections.[34]

The drastic change in silhouette was largely motivated by Paris's desire to assert its authority as fashion's leading tastemaker, especially as America – its largest and most important customer – was questioning it. The all-consuming nature of war left little room for Parisian women to indulge in the whims of fashion, which left the couturiers almost entirely dependent on their foreign buyers, especially the American department stores that purchased and licensed designs for reproduction.[35] But many in the American fashion industry questioned how Paris would fulfil the orders placed for the Autumn 1914 collections with limited access to supplies and materials. It was a valid concern, since numerous textile factories in the north were dangerously close to the war zone. To remain afloat, the Paris houses needed to reassure American buyers not only that their wartime orders would be fulfilled, but also that Parisian couture would continue its operations unscathed.

Paris couturiers equally needed and feared America. The industry's compromised position was an opportunity

George Barbier, *Le Bonheur du Jour* (The Happiness of the Day), 1920; plate 5, 'Love Is Blind'. George Barbier captured post-war *joie de vivre* in this plate. The inclusion of a group of doves in flight at the upper right-hand corner symbolizes the return to a period of peace and gaiety, underscored by the joyful attitudes of the plate's subjects. The four women exemplify the new modern ideal with their bobbed hair and carefree demeanour. Their lithe bodies under soft, romantic dresses are uncorseted, and hemlines have risen to just below the knee.

for a blossoming American fashion movement to gain momentum. The editor of *Ladies' Home Journal*, Edward Bok, had been promoting 'American fashion for American women' in the magazine since 1910, and in 1913 had collaborated with the *New York Times* on the first ever national American fashion-design contest, with great success. In the early months of the war, the newspaper confidently declared: 'Now is the time for Americans to design new fashions.'[36] In December 1914 *Vogue* sponsored a 'Fashion Fête', a fundraiser for the war that featured American designers exclusively. Parisian couturiers were outraged at what they regarded as blatant encroachment on their territory; competition with American designers, they felt, could be disastrous for an already fragile industry. But the threat was not to last, and transatlantic fears were laid to rest by the end of the year. 'I could not know then', wrote the editor of *Vogue*, 'that after the first frightening months the French couture would resume virtually normal production.'[37] *Vogue* staged a second Fashion Fête in November 1915, but this time in support of Parisian couture; eleven couturiers contributed models. Paris maintained its role as the world's fashion leader with America's unerring support.

Throughout the war, two seemingly polar opposite concepts – luxury consumption and wartime deprivation – were mitigated in the name of patriotism. France's luxury fashion industry had been a symbol of national pride since the days of the Sun King, Louis XIV. The vitality of its couture validated France's continued dominance as a world leader in culture and taste despite the war, its survival a

testament to France's strength and perseverance in the face of great suffering and loss. In the press and on the home front, fashion and war were intimately intertwined. To the American clientele, to purchase couture was to support France, while Parisian couturiers offered entire floors in their couture houses to the Red Cross, and the employees of others, such as Paquin and Poiret, made bandages for soldiers.[38] Lucile moved to New York City specifically to focus on business sales there, so as to support the Paris branch of her house.[39] Even the couture-house seamstresses, the iconic *midinettes* and some of the lowest-paid staff, agreed to half pay and shorter hours in the wake of the outbreak of war.[40]

With so many able-bodied men away at war, female workers were indispensable contributors to France's economy. As exemplified by the couture industry alone, women already constituted a substantial part of France's workforce, but the war necessitated the influx of hundreds of thousands more, many of whom filled jobs that had once been held exclusively by men. Women drove ambulances and cabs, and became tram workers, mail carriers and carpenters. The image of the trousered *munitionette*, soon rivalling that of the fashionable *midinette*, was fraught with controversy over women's new roles, which operated outside society's strict gender codes.[41] War work crossed class boundaries, too. 'The new occupation: ladies of France ministering to the wounded in a salon more familiar with the gaieties of peace than the grimness of war', wrote London's *Illustrated News*. 'Delicate hands which seemed made to be kissed by couturiers have found finer use.'[42] Society mavens and beloved stage actresses managed charities and canteens, turned their homes into hospitals or even became nurses themselves. The Red Cross nurse was a ubiquitous image of self-sacrifice and patriotism during the war years. 'Women were standing shoulder to shoulder with men and, as one after another was absorbed into some sort of War-work, the clothes became practical', wrote Lucile. 'Fashions became almost like the uniforms the men were wearing.'[43] For the hundreds of thousands of working women in France, comfort and utility of dress were key.

The Parisian wartime mode was marked by sober simplicity. Tailored suits became de rigueur. A sombre palette of neutrals, khakis, blues and blacks replaced the vivid and riotous colours that had immediately preceded the war. Women were encouraged to shy away from elaborate, showy fashions; the selection of 'serious clothes' for 'serious times' was a matter of practicality *and* patriotism.[44] The sombre colours were also reflective of a modified form of mourning across France, as strict customs crumbled in the face of such universal loss: 'Women felt, and rightly, that the indulgence of personal grief, even to the extent of wearing mourning, was incompatible with their duty to themselves, to their country, and to the men who cheerfully laid down their lives.'[45]

The Armistice was declared on 11 November 1918, and with it ended one of the greatest human tragedies of the 20th century. 'Bells were rung, cannon boomed, groups of strangers formed on the street corners, hugging and kissing each other. . .In the space of twenty-four hours the heart of our beautiful Paris began to beat again.'[46] After four years of struggle, Paris, in common with everywhere involved in the conflict, slowly began to pick up the pieces, but life was irreversibly altered, and with it women's fashion. The harsh reality of four years of war had left little room for the elaborate female toilettes and customs of the pre-war era: '[Women's] life has become so active, so full of sudden trips in ambulances, and engagements at hospitals and at all sorts of military organizations[,] that. . .anything that simplifies life is welcome', observed *Vogue*.[47] The trend for bobbed hair was perhaps most exemplary of the changed attitudes to personal appearance after the war, but also clothing that hung away from the body and promoted ease of movement and comfort above all else.

Lucile credited fashion's drastic simplification to a united effort by couturiers who, just as they had before the war, conspired to impose a new, minimalist silhouette on their clients in an effort to reduce production costs.[48] The couturière Coco Chanel would become the apostle of the 'pauvre luxe' look with her simple but chic – and deceptively expensive – sportswear, turning essentially practical clothing into a multibillion-dollar empire for which she is still remembered today. The changes in fashion were the result of a multitude of factors, over which the dictates of women's modern lifestyle arguably reigned supreme: 'The wiser

creator of woman's apparel has concentrated on wearable models which are easy to put on and easy to wear', observed *Vogue*, 'such as his modern client prefers to all others.'[49]

By early 1919 Parisian nightlife was again in full swing, with renewed vigour and spirit. Venues such as the theatre, opera and races were packed, but 'nothing in Paris is more alive than the Dance', observed *Vogue*, 'and nothing at the dance is more alive than the fringes.'[50] Women shed their wartime inhibitions and danced to the sounds of jazz music, to usher in the grand 1920s. It was in this atmosphere of post-war revelry, a time of prosperity and an almost frenzied pursuit of pleasure and luxury, that the pochoir technique was revived.

Gazette du Bon Ton returned (a controlling interest in it had been purchased by the magazine magnate Condé Nast during the war), as did *Modes et Manières d'Aujourd'hui*. Two new fashion and lifestyle periodicals, *Le Goût du Jour* (1918–22) and *Feuillets d'Art* (1919–22), were also published in pochoir, as was the album *La Dernière Lettre Persane* by the fur designer Fourrures Max, in 1920. *Monsieur*, a men's fashion magazine with pochoir plates, also debuted that year; it is still in production to this day, *sans* pochoir.

CONCLUSION

The work of the many artists seen in the spectrum of pochoir fashion publications produced between 1908 and 1925 represents a significant cross-section of contributors to the style of illustration that came to be referred to commonly as Art Deco. Today, Art Deco is synonymous with the 1920s, thanks in part to the Exposition Internationale des Arts Décoratifs et Industriels Modernes of 1925, from which the term was coined in the 1960s.[51] In truth, many of the characteristics commonly associated with Art Deco – ornamentation, exoticism, simplified geometric forms – were developed before World War I, when the exhibition itself was originally planned; a more fitting moniker for this specific pre-war style might be Art Moderne – a term that is especially applicable to fashion illustration. The mimicry of the distinctive styles of Art Moderne fashion illustrators in mass-produced fashion magazines – and also their work as illustrators for books of literature and poetry, as well as set and costume designers for theatre and film – disseminated their influence beyond fashion, and ultimately propagated the visual aesthetic of the Art Deco era that followed.

As the work became a more and more recognizable part of the public consciousness, the once novel, modern effects employed in fashion illustration became commonplace. By 1922 *Gazette du Bon Ton* had slowly begun to replace pochoir with colour lithography, a move that undoubtedly resulted in the demise of the publication. The magazine ended in 1925, its artistic integrity, rooted in the beauty of its hand-stencilled pochoir plates, entirely compromised. Three pochoir magazines that began in the 1920s, *Très*

Parisienne, *Les Idées Nouvelles de la Mode* and *Art, Goût, Beauté*, also attest to the decline of the technique. All three represent regression to standardized representations of fashion, while their execution of pochoir is below par. The collusion between art and fashion gradually lost potency, until it was replaced by the very type of hackneyed, overt commerciality that Paul Poiret detested. Fashion photography, which had begun to develop as a modern artistic medium in its own right as early as 1911, rendered fashion illustration almost entirely irrelevant.[52]

At the height of its popularity, it is believed that there were over thirty studios dedicated to pochoir production in Paris alone, but after World War II, demand for the technique went into steady decline.[53] By 1975 only a few studios produced pochoir, which was by then dubbed 'a poor relation among present-day graphic arts'.[54] In parallel, throughout the 1920s, the luxury fashion publication became increasingly obsolete, a fate that was solidified by the Great Depression. The Golden Age of pochoir in fashion illustration was therefore confined to a brief – albeit prolific – window of time straddling World War I, never to be rivalled.

1. Paul Adam, *The 1915 Mode as Shown by Paris: Panama Pacific International Exposition* (New York, 1915), 5–6.
2. George Barbier, *Pochoir: An Article from Arts et Metiers Graphiques Paris, 1937* (Pasadena, CA, 2000), 3.
3. Gerald W. R. Ward, ed., *The Grove Encyclopedia of Materials and Techniques in Art* (New York, 2008), 614–16.
4. Edward Greey, 'Japanese Stencils', *The Decorator and Furnisher*, August 1885, 150.
5. It must be clarified that the printmaker André Marty is not the illustrator André Édouard Marty.
6. Charles Rahn Fry, 'The Stencil Art of Pochoir', in *Pochoir by Painters: An Exhibition of Books, Folios, Prints, and Ephemera, 1918–1938 from the Collection of Charles Rahn Fry* (New York), 6.
7. *Pochoir*, 4.
8. Jean Saudé, *Traité d'enluminure d'art au pochoir* (Paris, 1925), 4.
9. *Ibid.*, 48.
10. See Harold Curwen's *Processes of Graphic Reproduction in Printing* (London, 1963) and Vance Gerry's *Pochoir: Practical Stenciling for the Modern Craftsman as Applied to Illustrations and Designs for Books &c.* (Pasadena, CA, 1991).
11. 'Biography', Daniel Jacomet website, www.danieljacometimprimeur.com (accessed 29 November 2014). The business passed to Jacomet's sons after his death in 1966, and then to his grandson Bruno in the 1980s.
12. 'Paul Poiret Here to Tell of his Art', *New York Times*, 21 September 1913, 11.
13. Palmer White, *Poiret* (New York, 1973), 31.
14. Paul Poiret, *King of Fashion: The Autobiography of Paul Poiret* (London, 2009), 36.
15. Edna Woolman Chase and Ilka Chase, *Always in Vogue* (New York, 1954), 35.
16. *King of Fashion*, 36.
17. 'Daring French Gown Again Wins Favor', *New York Times*, 17 May 1908, C1.
18. *Ibid.*
19. Cecil Beaton, *The Glass of Fashion* (London, 1954), 109–10.
20. Claude Lepape and Thierry Defert, trans. Jane Brenton, *From the Ballets Russes to Vogue: The Art of Georges Lepape* (London, 1984), 43.
21. *Always in Vogue*, 113.
22. 'Beau Brummels [*sic*] of the Brush', *Vogue*, 15 June 1914, 37. Equally significant to Chase was that the majority of the 'Beau Brummels' had studied under the same professor at L'École des Beaux-Arts, Fernand Cormon.
23. *Ibid.*, 35.
24. Lucile Duff-Gordon, *A Woman of Temperament* (Oxford, 2012), 182 (originally published as *Discretions and Indiscretions* by Jarrolds Ltd, London, in 1932).
25. William Griffiths, *The Great War* (New York, 2003), 6.
26. Ernest L. Bogart, *Direct and Indirect Costs of the Great War* (New York, 1920), 269–82. This astronomical number of soldiers dead combined 'actually known dead' and 'presumed dead'; the latter included missing and imprisoned soldiers.
27. *The Great War*, 172.
28. The government mandated the closure of all places of entertainment, shutting down cafés, opera houses, theatres and music halls. This left 75,000 Parisian men and women unemployed. Françoise Thébaud, *La Femme au temps de la guerre de 14* (Paris, 1986), 226–29.
29. Anne Rittenhouse, 'Couturiers under Arms', *Vogue*, 15 October 1914, 44, 45, 118.
30. Maude Bass-Krueger, 'From the "*Union Parfaite*" to the "*Union Brisée*": The French Couture Industry and the *Midinettes* during the Great War', *Costume*, 47, no. 1 (2013), 32.
31. 'Sweeping Changes in Garments Decreed by Paris', *New York Times*, 13 September 1914, SM9.
32. 'From the "*Union Parfaite*"', 32. Other houses that remained open to exhibit their Autumn 1914 collections included Premet, Drecoll, Bernard and Redfern. In 1915 twenty-one foreign couture houses operating in Paris, including the Austrian house Drecoll, were expunged from the Chambre syndicale in an effort on the part of the French to nationalize the industry.
33. While this shift in silhouette has commonly been ascribed to the need to free women from physically restrictive pre-war styles, so that they could engage in wartime work, such as nursing and other critical vocations left vacant by men at the Front, the image on page 170 confirms that skirt silhouettes were already travelling away from the body before the war. This plate, from 1914, depicts a sheer A-line skirt worn over a narrow, body-conscious sheath.
34. Anne Rittenhouse, 'Fashion under Fire', *Vogue*, 1 October 1914, 40, 41, 110.
35. Henri Bendel, 'The Adaptation of Fashions to the American Woman', *Harper's Bazaar*, June 1916, 64–65.
36. 'Now is the Time for Americans to Design New Fashions', *New York Times*, 27 September 1914.
37. *Always in Vogue*, 117. The American designer would continue to gain ground in the 1920s and 1930s, but it would not be until World War II, when Paris fell under German control, that American designers would truly gain their opportunity to design without the influence of Paris.
38. 'Paris in the Guise of the Red Cross', *Vogue*, 15 December 1914, 23–24.
39. *A Woman of Temperament*, 183.
40. Margaret Darrow, *French Women and the First World War: War Stories of the Home Front* (New York, 2000), 194.
41. *Ibid.*, 192.
42. 'The Paris Season, 1915: The Life of the French Woman of Fashion in War', *Illustrated London News*, 10 April 1915, 468–69.
43. *A Woman of Temperament*, 250.
44. 'Paris Holds Openings Despite War', *New York Times*, 28 February 1915.
45. 'War Mourning in Europe and America', *Vogue*, 15 June 1918, 30–33. The article questioned whether American women (the USA having joined the war in 1917) would 'abolish mourning during the war, as many Englishwomen have, or, like the Frenchwomen, wear a lighter mourning than formerly'.
46. 'C'est la Victoire', *Vogue*, 1 February 1919, 33–35.
47. 'The Fashion Fads of Paris', *Vogue*, 1 December 1918, 40–42.
48. *A Woman of Temperament*, 26.
49. 'The Premiere of a Paris Mode', *Vogue*, 1 April 1921, 32.
50. Francis de Miomandre, 'Paris Dances to the Pipes of Peace', *Vogue*, 15 April 1919, 69, 112.
51. Eric Myers, 'Art Deco: Still Not Forgiven for Being Fun', *New York Times*, 27 August 1995, H32. The historian Bevis Hillier popularized the term 'Art Deco' in his book of that title in 1968.
52. The birth of modern fashion photography is commonly ascribed by historians to the edition of *Art et décoration* of April 1911, which features a substantial spread of photographs of Poiret's latest designs, and constitutes Edward Steichen's debut as a fashion photographer. It was more than ten years before Steichen accepted another job as a fashion photographer for *Vogue* and *Vanity Fair*, in 1922.
53. Dale Roylance, *Art Deco Prints 1900–1925* (Princeton, NJ, 2000), 6. Major pochoir studios included Greningaire et Fils, Ranson et Fils, Charpentier, Beaufumé, Jacomet, Draeger Frères and of course the atelier of Saudé.
54. 'L'Enluminure au pochoir, un art méconnu', *Nouvelles de l'estampe*, 21 (May–June 1975), 9–15.

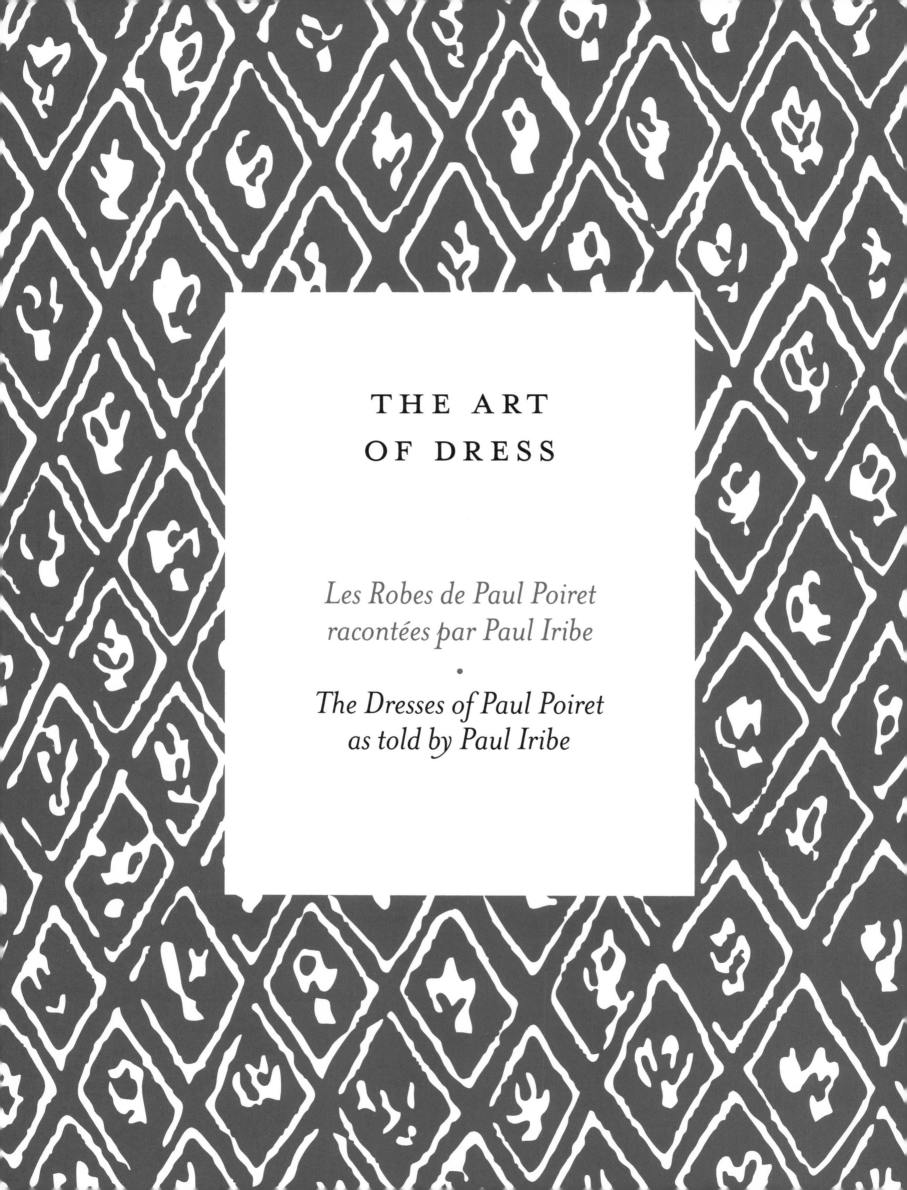

THE ART OF DRESS

Les Robes de Paul Poiret
racontées par Paul Iribe

·

The Dresses of Paul Poiret
as told by Paul Iribe

1

'Am I a fool when I dream of putting art into my dresses, a fool when I say dressmaking is an art?...
For I have always loved painters, and felt on an equal footing with them.
It seems that we practise the same craft and that they are my fellow workers.' Paul Poiret, 1930[1]

The fashion pioneer Paul Poiret set a new standard for the presentation of fashion illustration in 1908 when he commissioned the artist Paul Iribe to illustrate a portfolio of his designs entitled *Les Robes de Paul Poiret racontées par Paul Iribe*. Poiret intended the album for the 'élite of Society' and declared it to be 'in homage to all the great ladies of the whole world'.[2] Only 250 copies of the luxury, limited-edition pochoir album were produced, most of them distributed to Poiret's affluent clientele at no cost.

With *Les Robes*, Poiret endeavoured to breathe new life into the time-honoured medium of the fashion plate, which had traditionally provided realistic, line-for-line representations of the latest styles. For him, to convey the exact placement of a button or seam was of little importance: 'A garment is like a good portrait – the expression of a spiritual state,' he told *Vogue* in 1909, 'and there are robes [dresses] that sing the joy of living as others that herald tragic ends.'[3] The highly stylized illustrations he produced with Iribe transcended the realistic interpretation of his gowns; instead, he sought to convey the essence of his garments as an artist would a mood or feeling. In this way, Poiret's thinking was akin more to that of an artist than to that of a mere dressmaker, and he actively cultivated the larger-than-life public persona of artist, tastemaker and connoisseur. Indeed, one could argue that Poiret was the first fashion designer to become a bona fide celebrity.

From the beginning of his career, Poiret was determined to set himself apart. In 1903, after five years at the distinguished couture houses of Doucet and Worth, he opened his own atelier on Paris's rue Auber, where his artistic inclinations began to take shape: 'It was here that I began to receive artists, and to create around me a movement,' he wrote later.[4] Away from the rue de la Paix, the epicentre of Parisian fashion, Poiret's atelier on the outskirts of Parisian society made a statement about the couturier he intended to be. Conformity would not be part of his vocabulary; if Poiret's clientele wanted his distinctive wares, they would have to travel to him. He moved his atelier twice before settling in 1908 in the Faubourg Saint-Honoré in a majestic 18th-century building on the avenue d'Antin (now known as the avenue Franklin D. Roosevelt), where he also lived. In his memoirs, he wrote light-heartedly of 'this pretension on the part of a dressmaker, who received his clients in a private house, without a shop-sign and without window display'.[5]

Les Robes was just one aspect of a strategic marketing campaign Poiret used throughout his career, in which he promoted himself and his work within the realm of the fine arts. As a collector and self-declared artist, Poiret steeped himself in the artistic and cultural milieu of Paris, and kept in his company a number of artists, for whom he was both patron and friend. They included such historically significant figures as Robert Delaunay, Kees van Dongen, Raoul Dufy,

IL A ÉTÉ TIRÉ DE CET OVVRAGE DEVX CENT CINQVANTE
EXEMPLAIRES SVR PAPIER HOLLANDE, MIS DANS LE
COMMERCE AV PRIX DE QVARANTE FRANCS L'VN,

JVSTIFICATION DV TIRAGE.

Above Paul Iribe, *Les Robes de Paul Poiret racontées par Paul Iribe*
(The Dresses of Paul Poiret as told by Paul Iribe), 1908; imprint page.

Opposite Paul Iribe, *Les Robes de Paul Poiret racontées par Paul Iribe*
(The Dresses of Paul Poiret as told by Paul Iribe), 1908; cover.

André Dunoyer de Segonzac, Marie Laurencin, Henri
Matisse, Amedeo Modigliani and Pablo Picasso.[6] Poiret later
considered his discovery and patronage of artistic talent –
he claimed to have made Segonzac, among others, famous –
to be one of the crowning achievements of his career.[7]

It was undoubtedly through his association with the
artistic avant-garde that Poiret came to know the artist Paul
Iribe, whose satirical magazine *Le Témoin* included the work of
many artists from Poiret's orbit. As a leading graphic artist
of the day, Iribe was probably familiar to Poiret through his
impressive body of work, which focused primarily on political
satire.[8] As a young man, Iribe studied under the architect
Réne Binet, while simultaneously developing his talent for
illustration by contributing to a variety of French humorous
publications. Iribe's early work for the humorist journal
Le Rire, which published his first illustration when he was
just seventeen, reflects an illustrative style that emphasized a
flat, two-dimensional perspective. It was a style undeniably
reminiscent of his predecessors, such as Aubrey Beardsley and
Henri de Toulouse-Lautrec (the latter of whom contributed
to *Le Rire* in the 1890s), whose styles were largely informed
by Japanese woodblock prints. Iribe was clearly not a fashion
illustrator, but, for Poiret, that was the point.

For *Les Robes de Paul Poiret*, Iribe successfully adapted his
illustrative style to a format that fitted Poiret's needs, while
not entirely betraying his comedic hallmark. Throughout
the album's ten pages, Iribe depicts Poiret's innovative
and imaginative designs on statuesque, engaging beauties
caught in contemplation or intimate conversation. Iribe's
humour reveals itself subtly in the witty undertones of

these intimate scenes. On page 27, for instance, the viewer
catches three women in conversation, their sly smiles
suggesting that they know something the viewer does not.
One page after another presents an inviting scene with a
different model, or group of models, set in a stylized black-
and-white interior against which the brilliant jewel tones of
Poiret's designs pop. While Poiret's penchant for the exotic
'East' reveals itself in his bold colour palette, turban-like
headdresses and three oversized 'Confucius' coats (see page
32), the most overt inspiration is distinctively Neoclassical.

Almost every model in *Les Robes* wears a narrow
headscarf wrapped around a curly, sculpted coiffure, both
distinctive elements of the Grecian style. The hairstyles are
accompanied by high-waisted 'Directoire Revival' gowns,
so called because of the silhouette's popularity during the
Directoire and Empire periods of the late 18th and early
19th centuries. (The waistline, which fell just under the
bust, of these columnar chemise gowns is still referred to
today as an 'Empire waist'.) The historical associations are
further aided by Iribe's clever juxtaposition of the gowned
figures with Directoire-style furniture; however, the most
obvious allusion appears in the final illustration, in which
Poiret's white 'Josephine' gown is shown in front of George
Romney's 18th-century portrait of Emma Hamilton (see page
33). It is a meaningful juxtaposition, for the reference both
to Empress Joséphine, the first wife of Napoléon Bonaparte,
and to Hamilton, the spirited artist's model and muse; both
ladies were early adopters of the chemise gown in the final
years of the 18th century.

The novelty of *Les Robes* made international headlines in
both England and America soon after the album's release.
Vogue highlighted the illustrations in a three-page article,
declaring them 'the newest thing in fashion plates'.[9] The
album's success was further recognized with its inclusion
in the annual Salon d'Automne exhibition in 1909. The
Salon was a distinguished forum for the leading avant-
garde artists of the day, and those who had previously
exhibited there included Henri Matisse, Paul Cézanne
and Raoul Dufy (Poiret's future collaborator). The album
was much admired by Poiret's contemporaries, not only
fashion designers, but also publishers, fine artists, interior
designers and architects, who soon adopted the pochoir
technique for their own deluxe volumes. The publication
of *Les Robes de Paul Poiret* was seminal in establishing pochoir
as the medium of choice for luxury artist books and
designer albums of the 1910s and 1920s.

1. Paul Poiret, trans. Stephen Haden Guest, *King of Fashion: The Autobiography of Paul Poiret* (London, 2009), 161.
2. *Ibid.*, 48.
3. 'Fashion: Ideals of Elegance in Dress', *Vogue*, 8 July 1909, 36.
4. *King of Fashion*, 29.
5. *Ibid.*, 48.
6. Nancy Troy, *Couture Culture: A Study in Modern Art and Fashion* (Cambridge, MA, 2003), 38.
7. *King of Fashion*, 50–52.
8. By the age of twenty-three, Iribe had 'provided twenty publications more than 800 designs and acquired the reputation with editors and journalists as a leading designer of humor and satire'. Raymond Bachollet et al., *Paul Iribe* (Paris, 1982), 38.
9. 'Fashion: Ideals of Elegance in Dress', 34.

PAUL
IRIBE

The Art of Dress

Paul Iribe, *Les Robes de Paul Poiret racontées par Paul Iribe* (The Dresses of Paul Poiret as told by Paul Iribe), 1908; plates 1 (opposite) and 2 (above).

Les Robes de Paul Poiret racontées par Paul Iribe

Paul Iribe, *Les Robes de Paul Poiret racontées par Paul Iribe* (The Dresses of Paul Poiret as told by Paul Iribe), 1908; plate 3.

Paul Iribe, *Les Robes de Paul Poiret racontées
par Paul Iribe* (The Dresses of Paul Poiret
as told by Paul Iribe), 1908; plates 4
(above), 5 (opposite) and 6 (overleaf).

The Art of Dress

Paul Iribe, *Les Robes de Paul Poiret racontées
par Paul Iribe* (The Dresses of Paul Poiret
as told by Paul Iribe), 1908; plates 7
(opposite) and 8 (above).

Above Paul Iribe, *Les Robes de Paul Poiret racontées par Paul Iribe* (The Dresses of Paul Poiret as told by Paul Iribe), 1908; plate 9.

Throughout his career and even today, Poiret's 'Orientalism' has often been credited to the pervasive influence of the Ballets Russes, which had taken Paris by storm shortly before World War I. Although Poiret acknowledges an appreciation for Léon Bakst's elaborate and ornate Eastern-inspired sets and costumes, and perhaps their unconscious influence, his predilection for Orientalist themes had shown itself as early as 1903 when he designed a black kimono-type

coat for the House of Worth. The coat was decried as 'a horror' by Worth's distinguished client, the Russian Princess Bariatinsky, but was reincarnated in various ways in Poiret's future designs, as seen in the coats shown here.

Opposite Paul Iribe, *Les Robes de Paul Poiret racontées par Paul Iribe* (The Dresses of Paul Poiret as told by Paul Iribe), 1908; final plate.

An extant version of Poiret's 'Josephine' dress (1907), illustrated here, is held in the collection of the Musée des Arts Décoratifs in Paris. Realized in ivory satin, it has a tunic of black tulle. Metallic gold braid forms a

spiral motif at the hem of the tunic, and appears as a finish at the neckline and the bottom of the sleeves.

The rose was the symbol of Poiret's house, appearing on his labels and stationery and even on gold signet rings worn by his granddaughters. When the rose of pink crêpe and green satin at the centre of the bust of the museum's dress began to deteriorate in the 1950s, it was decided to restore it, since it was such a significant motif.

POIRET'S
NEW KINGDOM

*Les Choses de Paul Poiret
vues par Georges Lepape*

·

*The Things of Paul Poiret
as seen by Georges Lepape*

2

'*Paul Poiret was one of the last great patrons who was enlightened enough to allow the artists complete freedom of expression.*' Georges Lepape[1]

In February 1911 Paul Poiret published a second deluxe album of his designs, *Les Choses de Paul Poiret vues par Georges Lepape*. In form and technique, the album both embraced and expanded on the precedents that Poiret himself had established with *Les Robes de Paul Poiret racontées par Paul Iribe* (1908; see chapter 1) for a new genre of premier fashion publications. As with *Les Robes*, Poiret paid homage to his artist collaborator in the title of the album, as well as employing the pochoir technique to translate the artist's original gouache renderings into print. In a significant departure from the exclusivity Poiret afforded his first album, however, *Les Choses* was published in a run of 1,000 copies, four times that of its predecessor. Some 700 copies were made available for sale to the general public (although at fifty francs, the album was hardly affordable to any but a wealthy few), and 300 special editions were numbered and divided between Poiret and his 'co-author', Lepape, to be given as gifts.[2]

Before meeting Poiret in 1910, the young Lepape had no experience in the graphic arts, let alone fashion illustration. A student of the prominent historical painter Fernard Cormon and a graduate of the prestigious École des Beaux-Arts in Paris, he had only just begun a promising professional career.[3] Perhaps it was no coincidence that the year in which Lepape celebrated the first acceptance of his work at the Salon d'Automne was the same year that Poiret invited him to a private mannequin parade of his designs. The 'unforgettable procession' in the intimacy of Poiret's couture house left a lasting impression on Lepape, who vividly recalled the experience years later to his son: 'The dresses all different but with a perfect uncluttered line, the ruby carpet littered with the coats the models let fall. Each wore a brightly coloured turban. . .I was dazzled and amazed by what was in effect a ballet performance for just the two of us.'[4] After the presentation, Poiret gave the awestruck Lepape a Chinese tassel, some fabric samples and complete artistic license to interpret his designs: 'Do what you want,' he told Lepape, 'but give me something that conveys your impression.'[5]

Lepape reproduced the tassel on the cover of the album (see overleaf). A stark opening image, it is nonetheless a fitting choice, both as a reference to Poiret's patronage and as a visual companion to the album's vague title, which translates as 'The Things of Paul Poiret'. As the juxtaposition suggests, the album is about more than just the pretty 'robes' of its predecessor, an implication reinforced by Lepape's inclusion of two plates devoted exclusively to accessories. More than the literal definition of *choses*, however, Lepape's other images would further illustrate what the title only suggests: a symbiotic relationship between fashion and interior design. Indeed, Poiret was the first couturier to place interior design within a broader definition of fashion. Well-dressed women, Poiret said later, 'are living examples of decorum'.[6]

Les Choses opens with a model dressed in a turban and white chemise gown. Her downcast eyes address the rose she holds in her hand, while the other hand pulls back a pink-and-blue-striped curtain, a subtle invitation into the world that lies beyond – a seductive dreamscape of Lepape and

Poiret's shared revelry. Similar scenes of intimacy are revealed throughout the album, all imbued with a tantalizing allure that would become one of Lepape's hallmarks. In one of the most erotic scenes of the album, a woman falls back on to a soft bed of pillows, her gown slipping from her shoulders, her neck arched and cheeks flushed in an apparent state of pleasure. Where Iribe's work for *Les Robes* communicates a subtle level of wit and humour, Lepape's scenarios emphasize the seductive and sensuous qualities of Poiret's designs, which included garments and accessories inspired by the romanticized ideals of the 'Orient' – a continued source of inspiration for the designer. Lepape, too, looked to Eastern influences, including Persian miniatures, but also Noh theatre and Japanese woodblock prints, the last two of which he had been exposed to as a young boy.[7]

In seven of the twelve illustrations, Lepape places his models in the rooms and gardens of Poiret's couture house, the recently renovated 18th-century building to which Poiret had moved in 1908, and the site of their fortuitous first meeting.[8] Designed and decorated by the architect Louis Süe, the carefully articulated spaces were, in effect, Poiret's fashion aesthetic incarnate: the walls, carpets and furnishings blended traditions of French Neoclassical design with his signature bold colour palette. Lepape frames Poiret's designs within a bright orange border, aligning them with the concept of *Gesamtkunstwerk* ('total work of art'), a concept the designer had encountered when visiting the workshops of the Wiener Werkstätte, the artistic avant-garde community founded in 1903 by Josef Hoffmann and Koloman Moser in Vienna. Inspired by their integration of design disciplines with an emphasis on handcraftsmanship, Poiret was determined to impart a similar orthodoxy to his business practice, and he opened his own decorative arts school, Martine, in June 1911, followed by a commercial atelier of the same name the following year.[9] That year he also launched the first designer perfume, Rosine, named after his eldest daughter.

In the years before World War I, Poiret continually placed himself at the cutting edge of modern fashion, as he consistently challenged and redefined the field.[10] Published almost two and a half years after *Les Robes*, *Les Choses* remained the second album of its kind. Poiret was the first designer to follow his own lead and present a fresh – and still unrivalled – interpretation of fashion positioned within the realm of the fine arts. In its presentation of the first fashion illustrations of Georges Lepape, the album also represents a seminal moment in the life of one of fashion's greatest luminaries. Lepape would become an internationally celebrated and sought-after illustrator, as well as a distinguished designer of sets and costumes for the theatre. Between 1916 and 1939, he contributed 114 covers to American, French and English *Vogue* alone, more than any other artist in the magazine's history.[11]

A month after the release of the album, Poiret exhibited *Les Choses* at the Galerie Barbazanges, an art gallery on the premises of Poiret's couture house.[12] The album's exhibition and circulation to a wider audience extended Poiret's – and subsequently Lepape's – exposure and influence beyond the small, exclusive realm of Poiret's elite clientele. This time, however, Poiret's album did not escape the attention of the enterprising fashion community, notably his fellow couturière Jeanne Paquin, who would soon employ Poiret's artistic discourse – and his artistic collaborators – for her own deluxe publication (see chapter 3).

1. Quoted in Claude Lepape and Thierry Defert, trans. Jane Brenton, *From the Ballets Russes to Vogue: The Art of Georges Lepape* (London, 1984), 37.

2. In his memoirs, Lepape remembers the proud moment when Poiret offered him his share of the copies and referred to Lepape as his 'co-author'. That Poiret valued the collaboration is further alluded to on the cover of the album, where Lepape's name is the same size as Poiret's, an honour not afforded to Iribe before him. *From the Ballets Russes to Vogue*, 40.

3. *Ibid.*, 18, 25.

4. *Ibid.*, 36.

5. *Ibid.*

6. Florence Hull Winterburn, Jean-Philippe Worth and Paul Poiret, *Principles of Correct Dress* (New York & London, 1914), 248.

7. *From the Ballets Russes to Vogue*, 16. Lepape's uncle was an early importer of Japanese woodblock prints into France.

8. In 1910 Lepape designed a label for Poiret's packing boxes that depicted the façade of his couture house; Nancy Troy, *Couture Culture: A Study in Modern Art and Fashion* (Cambridge, MA, 2003), 174.

9. Paul Poiret, trans. Stephen Haden Guest, *King of Fashion: The Autobiography of Paul Poiret* (London, 2009), 83–85.

10. Poiret's integration of artistic discourse into the advertising of his house, and his expansion into interior design and perfume, was the blueprint for today's fashion industry and the prevalent concept of 'lifestyle' branding as employed by designers from Ralph Lauren to Chanel; Harold Koda and Andrew Bolton, 'Preface: The Prophet of Simplicity', in *Poiret* (New York, 2007), 13. For a detailed study of how Poiret and other couturiers appropriated artistic discourse into their business practices, see *Couture Culture*.

11. *From the Ballets Russes to Vogue*, 128.

12. *Ibid.*

LES CHOSES DE PAVL POIRET VVES PAR GEORGES LEPAPE

Georges Lepape, *Les Choses de Paul Poiret vues par Georges Lepape* (The Things of Paul Poiret as seen by Georges Lepape), 1911; cover (detail).

When Paul Poiret converted a grand building on the avenue d'Antin into his couture house, he asked his architect, Louis Süe, to incorporate a small proscenium stage for the presentation of fashion shows. At this time, catwalk shows were a relatively new phenomenon in France, something that was remarked on by the French fashion magazine *Femina* in December 1911: 'Most of the great Parisian couturiers have installed in their hotels a veritable theatre on which models, dressed in the latest styles, can turn at ease to show off to the best advantage the thousand and one details of the dress being launched. . .Clients, couturières and mannequins all enjoy this new innovation.' Paris couturiers took their cues from American department stores, which had been staging catwalk shows as elaborate spectacles at least since 1908, but the French adapted the show as an intimate experience for their clients. It was probably such a *mise-en-scène* that inspired Georges Lepape to create this plate of a woman in a simple white dress emerging from between two striped curtains to face an admiring audience.

Les Choses de Paul Poiret vues par Georges Lepape

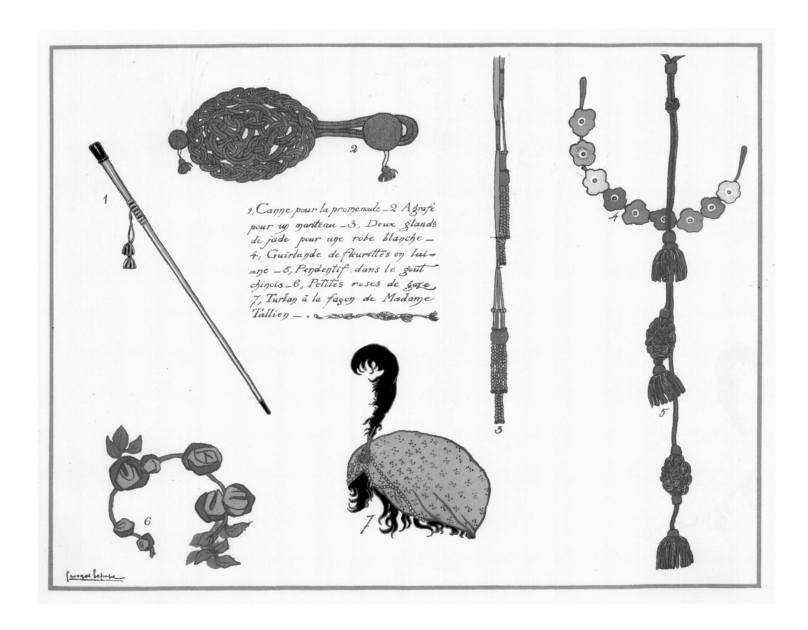

1, Canne pour la promenade _2 Agrafe
pour un manteau _3, Deux glands
de jade pour une robe blanche _
4, Guirlande de fleurettes en laine _5, Pendentif dans le goût
chinois _6, Petites roses de gaze
7, Turban à la façon de Madame
Tallien _ .

Previous page Georges Lepape, *Les Choses de Paul Poiret vues par Georges Lepape* (The Things of Paul Poiret as seen by Georges Lepape), 1911; plate 2.

The interiors of the Poiret couture house, designed by Louis Süe, were in a style that combined Neoclassical design motifs – such as floral rondels and the swagged garlands seen in this room's upper frieze – with clean, modern geometry and unexpected colour combinations. An article in *Le Miroir des Modes* in June 1912 on Poiret's couture house almost certainly describes the room featured here: 'The walls, decorated with panels of Nile green, are enriched by frames threaded with dark green and antiqued gold. On the floor, a raspberry-coloured carpet[;] on the windows, taffeta curtains in the same tone. The very clear opposition of these colours, the one neutral and the other hot, produced a bizarre atmosphere, at once soft and vibrant, and which must harmonize happily with the

fresh and buoyant colours from which Poiret likes to take his effects.' While the raspberry colour is only hinted at through the window at the back, the article speaks to the manifestation of Poiret's attempt to harmonize interior decor and fashion design, something he would develop further with the opening of his interior-design business Martine the same year.

Above Georges Lepape, *Les Choses de Paul Poiret vues par Georges Lepape* (The Things of Paul Poiret as seen by Georges Lepape), 1911; plate 4.

Opposite Georges Lepape, *Les Choses de Paul Poiret vues par Georges Lepape* (The Things of Paul Poiret as seen by Georges Lepape), 1911; plate 3.

Overleaf Georges Lepape, *Les Choses de Paul Poiret vues par Georges Lepape* (The Things of Paul Poiret as seen by Georges Lepape), 1911; plate 5 (detail).

Georges Lepape

Georges Lepape, *Les Choses de Paul Poiret vues par Georges Lepape*
(The Things of Paul Poiret as seen by Georges Lepape), 1911;
plates 6 (opposite) and 7 (above).

With the exception of the four women depicted in the final
plate of the album, every single model in *Les Choses de Paul Poiret*
is wearing a turban – a nod both to Poiret's Orientalist leanings
and to his supposed aversion to hair, which (according to

Lepape) he 'hated'. Poiret's close-fitting turbans stood in
direct contrast to the excessively wide-brimmed hats of the
period, while prefacing the ubiquitous cloche hat of the 1920s.
The close-up portrait opposite most certainly depicts Poiret's
free-spirited wife, Denise, who, as his model and muse, was a
walking advertisement for his most avant-garde designs.

Georges Lepape, *Les Choses de Paul Poiret
vues par Georges Lepape* (The Things of Paul
Poiret as seen by Georges Lepape), 1911;
plates 8 (above) and 9 (opposite).

Georges Lepape, *Les Choses de Paul Poiret vues par Georges Lepape* (The Things of Paul Poiret as seen by Georges Lepape), 1911; plate 10.

Left Georges Lepape, *Les Choses de Paul Poiret vues par Georges Lepape* (The Things of Paul Poiret as seen by Georges Lepape), 1911; plate 11.

Opposite Georges Lepape, *Les Choses de Paul Poiret vues par Georges Lepape* (The Things of Paul Poiret as seen by Georges Lepape), 1911; plate 12.

A singular attribution for innovations in fashion is often difficult to pinpoint; it is common for several designers, sensing the spirit and mood of the epoch, to find inspiration along similar lines. Poiret and Lucile both claimed to have invented the hobble skirt, for instance, just as Georges Lepape claimed that his wife gave Poiret the idea for his controversial *jupe-culotte* (literally 'skirt-trouser') featured here. After presenting Poiret with his wife's designs, Lepape claimed the designer told him to return 'in a week and you'll see your designs on my mannequins. You have just given me the idea for a divided skirt.' Lepape's claim aside, the *jupe-culotte*, referred to in the English and American press as 'Turkish trousers' and the 'harem skirt', caused international controversy. Many felt that the bifurcated garments challenged traditional gender roles, although Poiret initially conceived the *jupe-culotte* as an alternative to fashionable at-home wear, which was not necessarily for public consumption.

Les Choses de Paul Poiret vues par Georges Lepape

QUEEN OF THE RUE DE LA PAIX

*L'Eventail et la
Fourrure chez Paquin*

·

*Fans and Furs from
the House of Paquin*

3

'This unnamed Art, "Fashion", is practised in different places in different ways, but I believe in our time Fashion can have its birth only in Paris. . .here certain daring artistic conceptions can be presented that would not be received elsewhere with like graciousness.' Jeanne Paquin, 1912[1]

Eight months after the release of *Les Choses de Paul Poiret racontées par Paul Iribe* (1911), the 'world's greatest fashion authority', couturière Jeanne Paquin, released her own *pochoir* album of designs for furs and fans.[2] In a move that was no doubt inspired by her 'ardent rivalry' with Poiret, Madame Paquin invited not one but three illustrators to collaborate on the creation of *L'Eventail et la Fourrure chez Paquin*: Paul Iribe and Georges Lepape – the artists behind Poiret's two pioneering fashion albums – and George Barbier, whose work had been publically exhibited for the first time that year.[3] Like Poiret, Paquin embraced the artistic avant-garde as a means of non-traditional advertising, and she used it repeatedly throughout her career to maintain visibility and relevance in the fast-changing modern world. As the world's largest couture house, Paquin relied on remaining at the cutting edge of fashion merchandizing for its continued success.

The house of Paquin opened its doors in Paris in 1891, just one month before the marriage of its twenty-one-year-old head designer, Jeanne Marie Charlotte Beckers, to the couture house's owner, Isidore Jacob. (Jacob's family, which was Jewish, had used the name Paquin since his youth, and he changed his name legally to Paquin in 1899.)[4] Together the couple built a fashion empire that eventually opened branches in London, New York, Buenos Aires and Madrid, and employed an estimated 2,700 workers. After Isidore's premature death in 1907, Paquin proved herself to be an excellent businesswoman in her own right. In 1911, the year in which *L'Eventail* was released, her business was valued at twelve million francs. Paquin's outstanding contributions to the French economy would be recognized in 1913 when she became the first woman to be awarded the prestigious *Légion d'honneur*.[5]

But the commercial success of the House of Paquin was not the only reason it was to be admired. For nearly three decades, Jeanne Paquin was considered the 'queen of the rue de le Paix', an arbiter of sophisticated French taste with her mastery of colour, her eye for layering fabrics and textures, and the skilful nuances of her embellishments.[6] She was one of several designers during the early 20th century who helped to usher the fashionable silhouette towards modernity. As early as 1905, Paquin began to experiment with raising the waistline of her gowns to just below the bust, an early harbinger of the Directoire silhouette 'launched' by Poiret in 1908. Despite being a recognized innovator in her field, Paquin's 'new and daring' designs were applauded for having 'the good sense never to be extreme'; in 1910 her rejection of the controversial *jupe-culotte* (literally 'skirt-trouser') style made headlines internationally.[7]

Whereas Paquin's classicizing, if innovative, designs had always aligned her work within an acceptable realm of polite taste, her collection of 1911 presented a foray into an Orientalist aesthetic that was entirely new for the house.

It was a venture that did not escape the notice of the fashion press: 'Whether it is because her period of mourning is over or whether she has become touched by the madness for barbaric coloring,' wrote the *New York Times*, 'this season she has gone in for gorgeous color schemes in a way that startled the public', something the journalist credits to the influence of Poiret.[8] The comparison could be drawn again when, a month later, Paquin's own blend of Orientalist and classicizing themes would play out within the pages of *L'Eventail*. The album's three illustrations of black and white furs merely hint at the boldly coloured gowns beneath, but their Orientalist influences are underscored by the models' curly-toed shoes and pointed, helmet-like headwear.

Printed in a limited edition of 300, *L'Eventail et la Fourrure chez Paquin* contains seven illustrations, alternating the more realistic renderings of Paquin's fur designs by an artist identified simply as 'CR' with fan designs by Lepape, Iribe and Barbier. While the album features two fashion illustrators made famous by Poiret (Lepape and Iribe), Paquin can take credit for introducing the world of fashion to the talents of George Barbier – the Neoclassical fan design he contributed may represent his first foray into the realm of fashion, a field in which he would remain deeply immersed until his death at the pinnacle of his career in 1932.[9] Many of the details of Barbier's private life remain a mystery, but his professional career is prolifically documented through his illustration work for books and fashion publications and his designs for theatre and film. Barbier was an avid student of history, having frequented museums, antiques shops and bookshops all his life.[10] This brought an imaginative and informed perspective to his work, a fact that is underscored by his impressive library and collection of *objets d'art*, to which three walls of his private studio were dedicated. The fourth wall, lit by a skylight, was left blank. According to Barbier's friend the writer Jean-Louis Vaudoyer, it was here that Barbier's creations took form: 'He no longer sees anything in front of him but his own dreams. Before catching them in flight . . .for a moment he watched them pass on the great screen

of the sky among clouds and sunbeams.'[11] References to Greek and Roman myth, Classical art and architecture, 18th-century interiors and the mysteries of the Orient may all collide within a single Barbier plate.

The two designs for fans created by Paul Iribe for *L'Eventail* constituted only one of the collaborations between Iribe and Paquin that year. Iribe designed approximately fifty costumes for the play *Rue de la Paix* – a satire of the French couture industry – all of which were realized by Paquin.[12] Indeed, Paquin's name would become synonymous with innovative marketing strategies that played out on an international stage. In 1913 she executed the sartorial visions of the artist Étienne Drian and the Ballets Russes designer Léon Bakst.[13] The same year, in London, to call attention to her newly launched line of *robes tango* (tango dresses), which had shorter hemlines for ease of dancing, Paquin organized 'Tango Teas' that were spectacles of music, fashion, dancing and the culinary arts.[14] In 1914 she sent a team of mannequins and one hundred designs to the United States for a cross-country tour. The mannequins captured the public's imagination when they wore Paquin's signature gowns with brightly coloured wigs, even while attending the theatre, off-duty.[15] This sort of strategic pageantry was part and parcel of the Paquin business model from the start; Monsieur Paquin was well known to tip off the fashion press when one of the house's designs was to be worn by an actress recruited for that purpose.[16]

Jeanne Paquin retired in 1920, having served as the first woman president of the French couture industry's governing body, the Chambre syndicale de la couture parisienne, during the difficult years of World War I.[17] A study of her impressive oeuvre tells the tale of her innate talent and signature style, which toed the line between the stately, aristocratic styles associated with her illustrious predecessor the House of Worth, and the trendy exoticism embodied by the spirited new up-and-comer Poiret. Yet today Paquin is all but forgotten, her prolific career overshadowed by those of her better-known male contemporaries.

The fact that Paquin, the era's largest couture house, has fallen into relative obscurity has been questioned by fashion historians, who suggest that it could be attributed dually to the fact that Madame left no autobiography (Poiret wrote several), and that she was a pioneering woman in her profession.[18] As an exemplar of the modern enterprising woman, Paquin, along with her female contemporaries – Jeanne Lanvin and Lucile, Lady Duff-Gordon – paved the way for female designers, such as Gabrielle 'Coco' Chanel and Madeleine Vionnet, who dominated fashion during the 1920s and 1930s.

Opposite Fashions by Jeanne Paquin, as illustrated in *Les Créateurs de la Mode* (1910).

Left Georges Lepape, *L'Eventail et la Fourrure chez Paquin* (Fans and Furs from the House of Paquin), 1911; plate 1.

1. Jeanne Paquin, 'Madame Paquin on "How I Create Fashions"', *Vogue*, 1 November 1912, 82.
2. *The Ladies' Home Journal*, September 1914, 58.
3. Nancy Troy, *Couture Culture: A Study in Modern Art and Fashion* (Cambridge, MA, 2003), 174. Troy cites 'La mille-et-deuxième nuit' (May 1912), an unidentified clipping, possibly from *La Vie parisienne*, in Paquin Publicity Album, Fashion Research Centre, Bath.
4. Jan Glier Reeder, 'The Touch of Paquin: 1891–1920' (Master's thesis, Fashion Institute of Technology, New York, 1990), 7. Neither partner was a stranger to Parisian haute couture: Jeanne had trained as a *midinette* at the prominent couture house Rouff, and Isidore had been a partner in a couture venture called Paquin Lalanne et Cie.
5. *Ibid.*, 28.
6. SEM [Georges Goursat], *Le Vrai et le Faux chic* (Paris, 1914), 37.
7. 'Poiret and Paquin Cling to Barbaric Colors', *New York Times*, 15 October 1911.
8. *Ibid.*
9. Hiroshi Unno, *George Barbier: Master of Art Deco* (Tokyo, 2011), 286. Still a student in 1910, Barbier is also thought to have designed a diadem for the jeweller Cartier in 1911. Which collaboration came first is unclear.
10. Gordon N. Ray, *The Art Deco Book in France* (Charlottesville, VA, 2005), 39. The two-volume catalogue of an auction of Barbier's library after his death attests to his wide-ranging connoisseurship.
11. Jean-Louis Vaudoyer, Henri de Régnier and Charles Martin, *George Barbier* (Paris, 1929), 48.
12. 'La Mode et les Modes', *Les Modes*, March 1912, 8.
13. 'Society: The Adored Gaby Deslys', *Vogue*, 15 October 1913, 43.
14. *The Touch of Paquin*, 23.
15. 'Paquin to Exhibit Here' *New York Times*, 13 February 1914.
16. *The Touch of Paquin*, 11.
17. *Ibid.*, 13. After Paquin's retirement, her assistant Madeleine Wallis took over as head designer of the house until 1937. The house remained open under different designers until 1954, when it merged with the House of Worth. Worth-Paquin closed in 1956.
18. Valerie Steele, *Women of Fashion: Twentieth Century Designers* (New York, 1991), 27. Both Reeder (see note 4) and Steele propose this idea.

Queen of the Rue de la Paix

Previous pages, left Paul Iribe, *L'Eventail et la Fourrure chez Paquin*
(Fans and Furs from the House of Paquin), 1911; plate 2.

This design for a fan by Paul Iribe bears the designation 'pinxt'
just below his signature at the lower left. As 'pinxt' is shorthand
for 'painted by', the inclusion of this term introduces the
possibility that the pochoir was coloured by the artist himself.

Previous pages, right Paul Iribe, *L'Eventail et la Fourrure chez Paquin*
(Fans and Furs from the House of Paquin), 1911; plate 7.

Opposite (left) Rosette, *L'Eventail et la Fourrure chez Paquin*
(Fans and Furs from the House of Paquin), 1911; plate 3.

Furs were part of many couture houses' collections, but
Paquin was especially renowned for its fur and fur-trimmed
coats. Ever the innovator, Paquin was the first couture house
to create a special cold room for storing exotic skins at the
perfect temperature. In the autumn of 1912, Paquin expanded
its operations to New York, opening the fur salon Paquin &
Joire on the famed shopping stretch of Fifth Avenue. Following
the death of Jeanne Paquin's husband, her half-brother Henri
Joire and his wife, Suzanne, had become her business partners,
and Suzanne played an active role in establishing the Paquin
brand abroad. The 'artistic furs' offered by Paquin & Joire
were advertised in *Vogue* on 1 December, 1913, as 'now directly
available to American women at a saving of import duty through
the founding of this establishment where a staff of Paquin
experts will reproduce models in the distinctive fashions
characteristic of their Paris salons'.

Rosette, *L'Eventail et la Fourrure chez Paquin* (Fans and Furs from the
House of Paquin), 1911; plates 5 (opposite, right) and 6 (left).

Overleaf George Barbier, *L'Eventail et la Fourrure chez Paquin*
(Fans and Furs from the House of Paquin), 1911; plate 4.

In 1911 the first exhibition of Barbier's work was held at the
Boutet de Monvel gallery. His eighty-two watercolours were
grouped into three categories: Greek dancers, dancers from
the Ballets Russes and 'Belles du Moment' – themes that the
artist would explore repeatedly throughout his prestigious
career. In the preface to the exhibition catalogue, the poet and
writer Pierre Louÿs praised Barbier as a 'true Greek'. Barbier
himself cites Greek and Etruscan art as a major influence,
in particular the Etruscan tomb paintings in Tarquinia, Italy,
which may have provided the inspiration for this particular
composition; both depict Classical nude dancers and highly
specialized musical instruments, such as the *diaulos* played by
the kneeling figure on the far left-hand side of the fan.

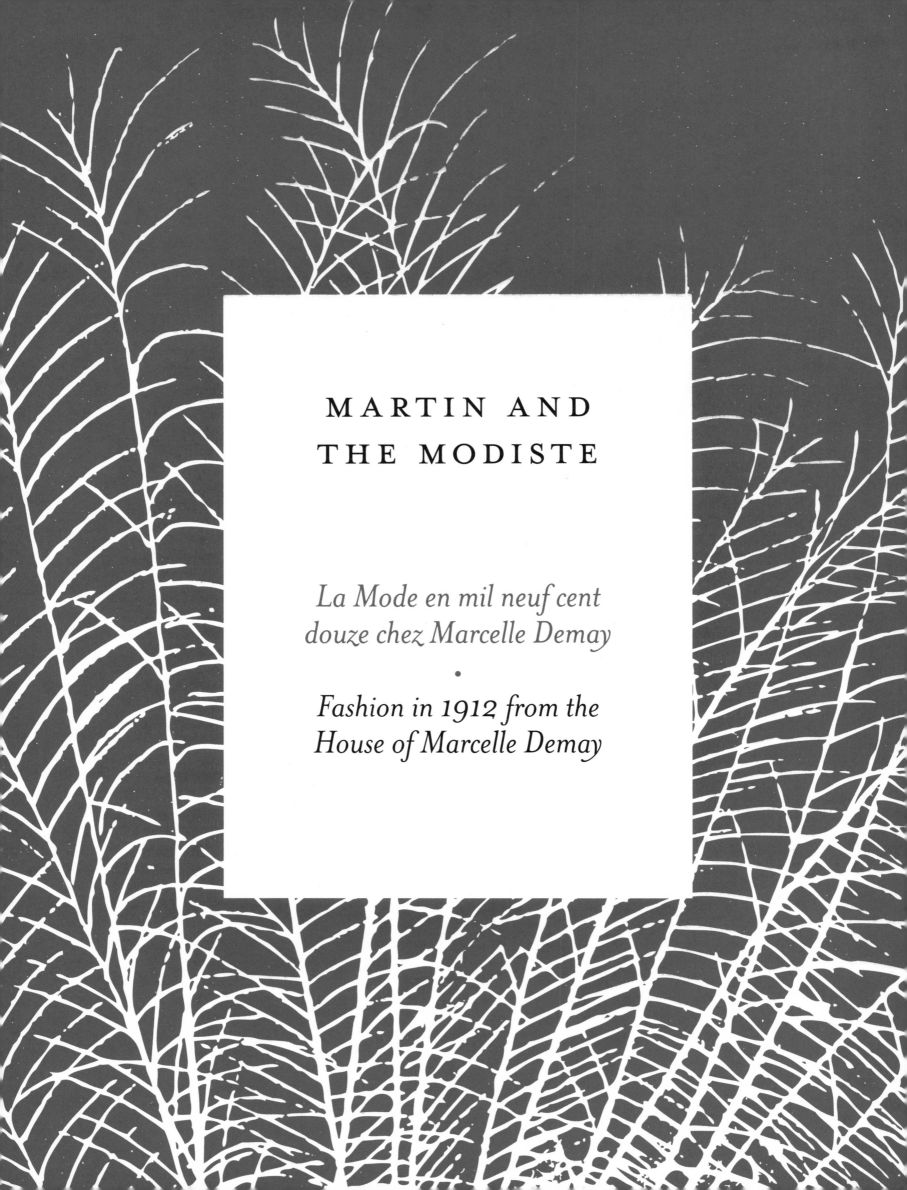

MARTIN AND THE MODISTE

La Mode en mil neuf cent douze chez Marcelle Demay

·

Fashion in 1912 from the House of Marcelle Demay

4

'*Paris is foremost in the search for the hat which all the world's a-seekin'* — *the hat which
makes women beautiful. Paris has found that hat; and Marcelle Demay is its creator.*'
John Wanamaker advertisement, 1911 [1]

When the *modiste* Marcelle Demay opened her atelier in Paris's fashionable rue Royale in 1910, the hat was an utterly essential – if not the single most important – element of a woman's dress. Strict codes of propriety dictated that any respectable woman, anywhere on the social spectrum, wear a hat with her daytime outing ensembles. In the most basic definition, a modiste was a milliner, but in France the term denoted more than a mere maker of hats: modistes were the haute couture designers of luxury headwear before World War I, and a revered component of the French fashion institution. [2] Demay and her contemporaries also sold purses, parasols and shawls among other necessary accoutrements to complete the fashionable woman's ensemble, but the hat was undoubtedly the *pièce de résistance*. 'The modiste is not a workwoman; she is a poet,' observed the writer and social commentator Octave Uzanne in 1912. 'The hat is a product of the imagination – a work of art, a poem of taste.' [3] Four of Demay's more whimsical and imaginative designs from that same year, one for each season, are featured in the album *La Mode en mil neuf cent douze chez Marcelle Demay* (Fashion in 1912 from the House of Marcelle Demay).

In a noted departure from previous pochoir fashion albums, Demay celebrated the 'Parisian of 1912' by alternating colourful pochoir renderings of her designs with black-and-white photographs of the hats themselves as modelled by the distinguished actress Berthe Cerny. The

illustrator Charles Martin used the vibrant possibilities of pochoir to imbue each hat with a unique, playful character. The bold flashes of colour impart a sense of life and movement to each of Demay's designs, an effect that is underscored by the apparent lightness and fragility of Martin's carefully articulated feathers. A photograph of the same hat modelled by the stately, albeit static, Cerny follows each pochoir. In this way, Demay reconciled Martin's stylized interpretation of her designs with the inherent commercial nature of the album. The tinted black-and-white photographs of the hats, worn with a complete ensemble and, more importantly, by a well-known actress, enforced both the desirability and the wearability of the designs to Demay's clients.

Demay's choice of Cerny was strategic. As the star of Henri Becque's aptly titled play *La Parisienne* at the Comédie-Française that year, Cerny was 'the perfect "Parisian" of the French theatre'; her high-profile role made her an ideal model for the album. [4] Demay was no stranger to the power of celebrity in advertising, nor was she averse to self-promotion. From the very beginning of her career, she had cultivated an international reputation as a premier millinery tastemaker. Demay had signed an exclusive contract with the American department-store giant John Wanamaker, which was selling advance models of her hats even before she opened her Paris atelier in the autumn of 1910. [5] Imported weekly, Demay's hats

MADEMOISELLE BERTHE CERNY
CRÉATRICE, À LA COMÉDIE-FRANÇAISE
DE ═══════════════
" LA PARISIENNE "
DE BECQVE
•
D'APRÈS LE TABLEAV DE JVLES CAYRON
CLICHÉ VIZZAVONA

kept Wanamaker clients abreast of the 'latest mode from Paris'. Furthermore, the appeal of her hats lay in their exclusivity. The store imported only a small selection of 'half-a-dozen' new styles every week, and assured its clients that 'the purchaser obtains the original and only model, as no copies are made in Wanamaker ateliers.'[6] Billed as the 'Real Paris of America', the Demay salons at Wanamaker were modelled on their Parisian counterpart. By invoking an aura of French sophistication in an arena most clearly associated with the mass market, in addition to maintaining the quality and originality of her creations, Demay was able to extend her influence beyond France without compromising the quality of her work or her integrity as a maker of luxury headwear. Wanamaker would remain the only purveyor of Demay designs in America throughout the 1910s.

It was not long after she signed the contract with Wanamaker that Demay's hats began to appear in the leading fashion magazines, including *Vogue*, *Les Modes* and, perhaps most surprisingly, the men's fashion magazine *Nos Élégances et la Mode Masculine*, which in 1911 began to highlight one design from both Demay and the couturière Jeanne Paquin in each issue. Demay's name made the cover of *Nos Élégances* in December 1911 in an illustration by Georges Lepape that depicts a woman wearing an Eastern-inspired ensemble à la Poiret, with a feathered turban presumably by Demay. That same year, Demay

produced an album entitled *Nos Étoiles* (Our Stars), which featured not one but eighteen of France's leading stage actresses modelling her designs. The album displays both Demay's meteoric rise to success – she had opened her atelier less than a year earlier, yet was now modiste to the 'Stars' – and the exquisite craftsmanship of a wide range of hats that presumably enticed her glamorous clientele. The largest, a wide, ostrich-plumed confection, is worn by the 'human aviary' Gaby Deslys, whose name would become synonymous with ostentatious, over-the-top headwear throughout the 1910s.[7]

Like *Nos Étoiles* before it, *La Mode en mil neuf cent douze* pays tribute to the beauty of feathers in fashion, its cover graced by a Martin illustration of a majestic, flying bird. However, a few of his other illustrations hint at a subject that was increasingly fraught with contention and controversy. Each photograph of Cerny is accompanied by a Martin illustration at the bottom of the page. In one, a woman dressed in the style of Greek antiquity contemplates the bird in her hand: friend or fashion accessory?, she seems to ask. The answer appears to be found above, quite literally, in Cerny's feathered hat. Another Martin illustration depicts a snake chasing two birds. Both illustrations are relevant allegories in the face of growing tension between wildlife activists and the feather trade. During a six-month period in 1911, four feather-trading firms sold a total of approximately

223,490 bird corpses in London alone.[8] By 1913 the controversy over the use of feathers in fashion, dubbed 'murderous millinery' in the press, had reached boiling point, with public outcry by activists and environmentally conscious citizens alike over the profligate killing of birds in the name of fashion.[9] 'The whole matter is up to the women,' wrote William T. Hornaday, director of the New York Zoological park and author of *Our Vanishing Wildlife* (1913). 'On their heads is the blood of the slaughtered innocents. Let those who are made indignant by the shameful facts of the case pledge themselves and one another to this cruel and wicked industry.'[10]

While Hornaday and his sympathizers in America and England called on women to boycott feathered hats, in France the literature on the subject was largely sympathetic to the feather trade.[11] Despite public outcry, it would appear that it was the caprice of fashion and the changing taste of the French modistes and their clientele that would shift taste away from large hats and their profligate consumption of feathers. In an article of 1913 entitled 'Modistes Declare the Survival of the Smallest', *Vogue* describes a hat that clearly prefaces the arrival of the ubiquitous cloche hat of the 1920s: 'a crownless turban, scarce more than a wreath of brown straw'.[12] As Poiret so aptly put it, 'every excess in matters of fashion is a sign of the end.'[13] The dramatic S-curve silhouette prefaced the demise of the corset, just as Demay's ornate confections in *La Mode en mil neuf cent douze* marked one of the last chapters in large, decadent headwear. The outbreak of World War I would furthermore ensure the survival of small, simple styles of headwear and clothing, as all excess was suppressed. The use of feathers, although greatly reduced, did not altogether disappear, and neither did Demay, who remained a prominent international figure in millinery throughout the war.

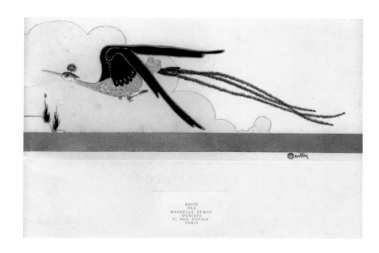

Opposite La Mode en mil neuf cent douze chez Marcelle Demay (Fashion in 1912 from the House of Marcelle Demay), 1912; title and imprint pages.

Right (above) Charles Martin, *Journal des Dames et des Modes* (Journal of Ladies and Fashions), 10 September 1912; plate 19, hats by Marcelle Demay.

Right Charles Martin, *La Mode en mil neuf cent douze chez Marcelle Demay* (Fashion in 1912 from the House of Marcelle Demay), 1912; cover (detail).

1. Wanamaker advertisement, *The Smart Set*, January 1911, 178.
2. 'Paris Millinery Dicta', *Vogue*, 1 April 1912, 26–27.
3. Octave Uzanne, *The Modern Parisienne* (New York, 1912), 103.
4. *La Mode en mil neuf cent douze chez Marcelle Demay* (Paris, 1912), 2.
5. Advertisement, *The Illustrated Milliner*, 5 August 1910, 18.
6. Wanamaker's remained the exclusive purveyor of Demay's hats in the United States until at least 1919.
7. Cecil Beaton, *The Glass of Fashion* (London, 1954), 41.
8. 'Murderous Millinery', *New York Times*, 31 July 1898, 15; 'Now for the Plumeless Hat: Tyrant Man Responsible for "Murderous Millinery"', *New York Times*, 23 April 1913, 3.
9. *Ibid.*
10. William T. Hornaday, 'Woman the Juggernaut of the Bird World', *New York Times*, 23 February 1913, 76.
11. Robin W. Doughty, *Feather Fashions and Bird Preservation* (Berkeley and Los Angeles, CA, 1974), 57.
12. 'Modistes Declare the Survival of the Smallest', *Vogue*, 1 April 1913, 23.
13. Paul Poiret, trans. Stephen Haden Guest, *King of Fashion: The Autobiography of Paul Poiret* (London, 2009), 156.

Opposite Talbot, *La Mode en mil neuf cent douze chez Marcelle Demay* (Fashion in 1912 from the House of Marcelle Demay), 1912; first photograph.

The use of an actress as model was a long-established and highly effective marketing strategy used by couturiers and modistes alike. In the nascent days of the cinema, the theatre was one of the foremost entertainment venues, and its actresses were international celebrities idolized by adoring fans. On and off the stage, actresses – next to couturiers'

mannequins and women of the demi-monde – were fashion's leading tastemakers: 'The launching of fashions is almost entirely in the hands of the three classes enumerated,' read an article on Paris fashion in *McClure*'s magazine in June 1914; 'it does not appear that there are any great ladies who can make or mar a fashion by a nod.' The demi-monde ('half-world') was a term used to refer to a liminal space within society inhabited by courtesans and actresses, who were frequently the mistresses of wealthy men. Showering one's lover publicly with apartments, jewels and haute couture

was accepted in France before World War I, and was even considered to be a measure of a man's financial and social success; demi-mondaines were therefore often at the absolute height of fashion.

Above Charles Martin, *La Mode en mil neuf cent douze chez Marcelle Demay* (Fashion in 1912 from the House of Marcelle Demay), 1912; plate 1.

Above Talbot, *La Mode en mil neuf cent douze chez Marcelle Demay* (Fashion in 1912 from the House of Marcelle Demay), 1912; second photograph.

At the height of the early 20th-century craze for feathers in millinery, a single exotic specimen could cost $75 (nearly $2,000 in today's dollars). A simple hat designed by a leading milliner would cost an average of $600 today, whereas an elaborate example came to well over $7,000. An article in the *New York Times* on 17 July 1910, entitled 'What Mrs. Million Pays for her Hats', noted that the prices of the best hats were the equivalent of the couture dress with which they were to be paired. It is estimated that women of substantial means spent $50,000–75,000 a year on millinery.

Opposite Charles Martin, *La Mode en mil neuf cent douze chez Marcelle Demay* (Fashion in 1912 from the House of Marcelle Demay), 1912; plate 2.

Talbot

Opposite Talbot, *La Mode en mil neuf cent douze chez Marcelle Demay* (Fashion in 1912 from the House of Marcelle Demay), 1912; third photograph.

Above Charles Martin, *La Mode en mil neuf cent douze chez Marcelle Demay* (Fashion in 1912 from the House of Marcelle Demay), 1912; plate 3.

The limitations of the photography available to Marcelle Demay during this period confined her brilliantly coloured creations to the realm of black and white. Instead of resorting to the more typical, but less effective, tactic of hand-colouring the photographs, she chose to illustrate the true, riotous colour palette of her confections in pochoir.

It is likely that many of the saturated hues and pale tinges found in Demay's hats, as seen here, were achieved using dye. A skilled dye artist was an invaluable asset to the milliner, and it was considered that the finest training was to be had in France: 'No American can do this work,' remarked the *New York Times* in 1910. 'The mixing of the dyes, the harmonizing of colors, the production of delicate, pale tints such as one sees in the evening sky or on the sea, require the skillful hand and artistic sense of the French-born.'

Above Talbot, *La Mode en mil neuf cent douze chez Marcelle Demay* (Fashion in 1912 from the House of Marcelle Demay), 1912; fourth photograph.

Opposite Charles Martin, *La Mode en mil neuf cent douze chez Marcelle Demay* (Fashion in 1912 from the House of Marcelle Demay), 1912; plate 4.

The gossamer wisps of the egret's feathers made them highly prized for use in millinery during this period. Eastern-inspired turbans used the tufted head-plumes or aigrettes of the egret so frequently that any sort of singular, vertical ornamentation on a turban, diadem or hat – including clusters of jewels – became known by that term. Here, Marcelle Demay sumptuously pairs an entire spray of costly egret feathers with another, equally coveted luxury material: chinchilla fur.

Martin and the Modiste

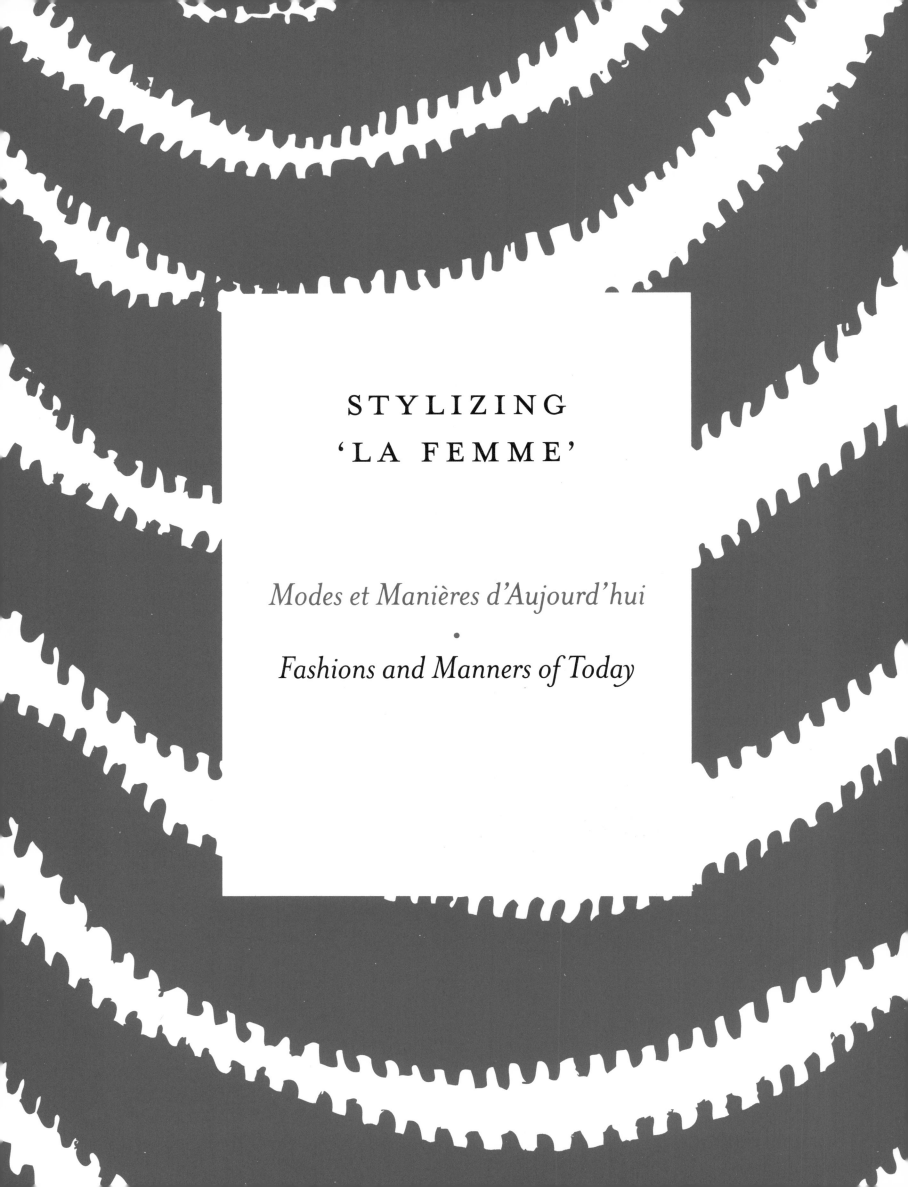

STYLIZING 'LA FEMME'

Modes et Manières d'Aujourd'hui

·

Fashions and Manners of Today

5

'Because the Woman is the eternal opportunity of art. . .you find her everywhere, a divine inspiration, an eternal object of our preoccupations, that we called her Isis, Mylitta, Ischuari, Aphrodite, the Virgin, or simply, as in our day, la Femme.' Pierre Corrard, 1912[1]

The poet and publisher Pierre Corrard was inspired to create the fashion almanac *Modes et Manières d'Aujourd'hui* after observing three fashionable women skimming stones on the beach. 'Their bodies were liberated from restraints and their dresses flourished,' he wrote in the preface to the first issue. 'Each of their attitudes was worth immortalizing.'[2] A self-proclaimed 'passionate admirer of women', Corrard envisioned *Modes et Manières* as an annual testament to the fashion and manners of the idealized *Femme*, interpreted through the vision of a single artist. He printed the album in a limited edition of 300, with the intention of courting a readership of only 'a small group of distinguished people', or, more presumably, a wealthy and sophisticated few who he felt could truly appreciate – and afford – the artistic nuances of his publication.[3] For the first issue, Corrard enlisted the talent of Georges Lepape, each of whose twelve illustrations is accompanied by Corrard's witty narrative: 'The Painter celebrates the form and colour, the Man of the Verb expresses the idea.'[4] This relationship would be maintained in all future incarnations of the publication, which similarly paired fashion illustration and literature's greatest luminaries. In total, seven issues were produced from 1912 to 1922, with a seven-year hiatus owing to World War I and the untimely death of its founder.

Corrard was the first of several publishers in 1912 to find romantic inspiration in the fashion journals of yesteryear. He based his publication on an early 19th-century annual entitled *Modes et Manières du Jour* (see overleaf). Published from 1798 to 1808, the series of fifty-two plates represents the artistic oeuvre of one man: the celebrated French artist and printmaker Philibert-Louis Debucourt. Corrard emulated not only Debucourt's title and visual layout, but also his artistic musings on contemporary life and fashion, the latter a 'science' that Corrard believed to be a neglected yet invaluable area of study. He recognized that clothing, in particular fashionable clothing, was revealing not only of the customs and manners of any given society, but also of the spirit of an era, as well as its artistic temperament. 'All the elegant epochs of *La Femme* were epochs of the flourishing of art,' he wrote, and 1912 was no exception.[5] This symbiotic relationship between fashion and art is at the core of *Modes et Manières d'Aujourd'hui*.

Corrard's choice of Lepape for the debut album, which was published on 9 May 1912, was no doubt two-fold. In Lepape, Corrard found both the visual counterpart of his literary skill – he called Lepape a 'poet of superb imagination' – and an artist intimately connected to the world of high fashion through his working and personal relationship with Paul Poiret.[6] Lepape's contribution to *Modes et Manières* was meant to summarize popular design traits, rather than replicate existing fashions, and yet the influence of Poiret is undeniable. Each of Lepape's scenarios, encased in an orange border and rendered in a bold pochoir palette, is unmistakably indebted to *Les Choses*

MODES ET MANIÈRES D'AUJOURD'HUI

1914

considered 'a decorator rather than an illustrator', as the scholar Gordon N. Ray so aptly put it: 'He did not see his work as an interpretation of the successive phases of the text before him. Instead he found in each subject which he isolated from the text an opportunity for creating a single perfect design.' It is this innate talent for imposing his own distinctive perspective on a text in place of a literal – and more traditional – interpretation that makes Barbier one of the defining illustrators of the Art Moderne and Art Deco eras.

The untimely death of Pierre Corrard, coupled with the outbreak of World War I (it is unclear if the two were related), suspended production of *Modes et Manières* indefinitely. The next issue did not appear until seven years later, in 1921, when it was revived by Corrard's widow and the publisher Jules Meynial. Perhaps in tribute to Corrard's debut album, Lepape was asked to illustrate the first post-war issue. His illustrations pay tribute to the persevering and indomitable spirit of *La Femme* during the war years, taking the reader from 'August 1914' to 'The Victory' in a notably evolved illustrative style. Lepape, who lasted only forty-eight hours in the army because of arthritis, had time to develop his style throughout the war years with numerous commissions for magazines including British *Vogue*, *Harper's Bazaar* and *Femina*, as well as costume design for the theatre.[10] In an obvious departure from his sumptuous, decadent depictions of pre-war French society, Lepape's images for the fourth issue of *Modes et Manières* reflect a broader trend in fashion illustration that embraced a severity of line and restrained use of colour. It was a development indicative of both the prevalence of Cubism in art and the changes in a society no longer tinted by Arabian fantasies; the effect of the war infiltrated every aspect of life, including fashion. 'Clothing clearly expresses the mentality of the people,' Corrard once wrote.[11]

The final three issues of *Modes et Manières d'Aujourd'hui*, although not without idealism, are devoid of romanticized, Orientalist notions. They instead posit a notably evolved and independent *Femme* within the framework of recognizable, archetypal settings. Men, if present at all, serve as mere backdrops to her carefree escapades. The illustrator André Édouard Marty paid homage to the end of the war in the fifth issue's opening image, 'The Demobilization', which depicts a father returning home to his family (see pages 98–99). As he sits wearing his army blues, each of his three children presents him with a piece of a civilian ensemble – an invitation back into a normal life. Marty is otherwise quick to dismiss any direct references to the difficult period; he was himself undergoing a period of convalescence after his service in the war.[12] (It is perhaps for this reason that his illustrations, dated 1919, were not published until 1921.) He chose instead to focus on the activities of women whose lives had returned to a sense of normality, and featured scenes such as dancing and attending fancy-dress parties.

de Paul Poiret, as are the turban-bedecked beauties in loose, flowing gowns to Poiret's revolutionary designs. Lepape similarly drew on the familiar interiors of Poiret's atelier for inspiration, as is evident in one plate featuring a bed of soft pink and orange cushions and another with a black-and-white chequered floor. 'Lepape will not deny the part I took in his work, and the influence I exercised over him,' Poiret would later say. 'His fine career has justified me.'[7]

For the second issue, published in June 1913, the illustrator Charles Martin presented his own unique perspective on the fashionable *Femme*. Martin's hourglass beauties move through a world of music, hunting and snowstorms, a more active alternative to the languorous Lepape ladies. An essay by Nozière on the state of fashion prefaces the illustrations: 'Today, the body tends to keep its lines, its liberty of movements. . . .Fashion delivers us today the secrets of a woman. She is as naked as a slave in a harem.'[8] While Martin, and Lepape before him, only hinted at such an exotic interpretation of women's fashion, George Barbier gave it free rein in his illustrations for the third issue of *Modes et Manières*, published on 2 March 1914.

Barbier unabashedly celebrated the naked body of *La Femme* in not one but three separate plates. His material, while undeniably provocative, is not definitively erotic, but is presented as part of a broader visual narrative – one so potent that Barbier's literary companion in *Modes et Manières*, the poet Henri de Régnier, was inspired to write his accompanying sonnets and poems only *after* viewing Barbier's illustrations.[9] It is for this reason that Barbier is

Stylizing 'La Femme'

Assertive, independent women are at the heart of Robert Bonfils's edition of *Modes et Manières* of 1922. In 'La Robe d'Amour' a scantily clad woman dresses, her exhausted lover asleep in the bed in the background, while in 'Le Bain' various women swim in body-baring swimming costumes (see pages 103 and 104). Perhaps tame by today's standards, the swimsuits depicted are the most revealing ever to have been worn at this point in fashion history. Other plates depict the assured swing of an experienced woman golfer and a woman horse-riding front – not side – saddle. Bonfils's self-sufficient women hint at the breakdown of gender and societal barriers after four years of war, their newly embraced roles and freedom clearly reflected in their clothing, with its shortened hemlines and lowered décolletage.

Fernand Siméon's illustrations for the seventh issue of *Modes et Manières* present an extreme contrast to the colourful, celebratory albums of his predecessors. Activities such as shopping and dancing, previously depicted as light-hearted and fun, are given new meaning at the hands of Siméon, whose thick, harsh black lines, printed with woodblocks, impart a sense of drama and unease. A monochromatic palette underscores the effect: only a single stencilled colour is used for each plate. Siméon's reductive style was mirrored by other illustrators such as Eduardo García Benito and Thayaht, who similarly emphasized line over a flourish of colour.

'I dreamed that it was a poem,' wrote Corrard about his conception of *Modes et Manières*, 'or more simply a book of hours, beautifully illuminated, which celebrated the woman, sovereign and victorious Divinity.'[13] Ten years after the debut of *Modes et Manières d'Aujourd'hui*, Siméon's issue marked the end of Corrard's masterpiece. The seven issues survive today as a testament to one man's vision, carried on even after his death.

Les Cerises.
(Coiffure en Cheveux et perles.)

Above Modes et Manières du Jour (Fashions and Manners of the Day), *c.* 1800; 'Cherries: Hairstyle with Pearls'.

Opposite George Barbier, *Modes et Manières d'Aujourd'hui* (Fashions and Manners of Today), 1914; cover.

1. Pierre Corrard, *Modes et Manières d'Aujourd'hui* (1912), 16.
2. *Ibid.*, 1.
3. *Ibid.*, 9.
4. *Ibid.*, 8.
5. *Ibid.*, 6.
6. *Ibid.*, 8.
7. Paul Poiret, trans. Stephen Haden Guest, *King of Fashion: The Autobiography of Paul Poiret* (London, 2009), 50.
8. *Modes et Manières* (1913), 5.
9. Gordon N. Ray, *The Art Deco Book in France* (Charlottesville, VA, 2005), 43.
10. Claude Lepape and Thierry Defert, trans. Jane Brenton, *From the Ballets Russes to Vogue: The Art of Georges Lepape* (London, 1984), 82, 89, 116.
11. *Modes et Manières* (1912), 3. More than Lepape's illustrative style had changed between 1914 and 1919. What was a necessity for the millions of active female workers and volunteers throughout the war had become fashion by the war's end: shortened hemlines, widened skirts and descending waistlines were part of a movement towards practical sportswear that would come to define modern fashion and the modern woman.
12. *From the Ballets Russes to Vogue*, 103. A fellow student of Lepape and Martin at the Atelier Cormon, Marty was a promising fashion illustrator before the war and a regular contributor to the luxury magazine *Gazette du Bon Ton* (see chapter 7).
13. *Modes et Manières* (1912), 3.

Est-elle aimable ou rébarbative? Nul n'en
Sait rien... à cause de son nez impertinent.

Ses doigts, selant ses mains sont fines.
Et de b... ...barrassées,
Ressembl... ... hermines
Dans d... ...ges embarrassées.

Et son geste lui-même a la joie d'un envol!

Previous pages (left) Georges Lepape, *Modes et Manières d'Aujourd'hui* (Fashions and Manners of Today), 1912; plate 1, 'The Toilette'.

In the first issue of *Modes et Manières d'Aujourd'hui*, Georges Lepape refers to the history of fashion plates with his inclusion of a Nubian servant boy, a familiar trope. Young male pages of assumed African or Middle Eastern descent are commonly shown attending to fashionable European women in 18th-century fashion plates. This motif was probably inspired by King Louix XV's mistress Madame du Barry, who took into service a seven-year-old Bengali boy named Zamor.

Previous pages (right) Georges Lepape, *Modes et Manières d'Aujourd'hui* (Fashions and Manners of Today), 1912; plate 2, 'The Interval'.

Left Georges Lepape, *Modes et Manières d'Aujourd'hui* (Fashions and Manners of Today), 1912; plate 3, 'The Butterflies'.

Above Georges Lepape, *Modes et Manières d'Aujourd'hui* (Fashions and Manners of Today), 1912; plate 8, 'Ermines'.

Opposite Georges Lepape, *Modes et Manières d'Aujourd'hui* (Fashions and Manners of Today), 1912; plate 12, 'Persian Dress'.

Georges Lepape.

La Mule

Ainsi le long des haies dansent les chevreaux.

Martin

Les Lucioles

Sur la grève où ses pas ont conduit son ennui, Qui sont les enfants des étoiles de la nuit,
Pour l'amuser les lucioles Lui dessinent une auréole.

La Neige

Quand aurez-vous fini, flocons qui floconnez,
D'assaillir, sans façon, le bout de notre nez !

The 1913 issue of *Modes et Manières d'Aujourd'hui* was illustrated by Charles Martin, a native of the south of France, who had made his way to Paris to study at the École des Beaux-Arts alongside Georges Lepape and George Barbier. Martin was one of the most prolific illustrators of the period, and contributed to a wide variety of French publications including books, fashion magazines, and collaborative projects such as the pochoir album *Sports et Divertissements* ('Sports and Leisure'), in which his illustrations accompany short musical pieces by the composer Erik Satie on that theme.

Previous pages (left) Charles Martin, *Modes et Manières d'Aujourd'hui* (Fashions and Manners of Today), 1913; plate 3, 'The Mule'.

Previous pages (right) Charles Martin, *Modes et Manières d'Aujourd'hui* (Fashions and Manners of Today), 1913; plate 8, 'The Fireflies'.

Above Charles Martin, *Modes et Manières d'Aujourd'hui* (Fashions and Manners of Today), 1913; plate 1, 'The Lady and the Parrot'.

Right Charles Martin, *Modes et Manières d'Aujourd'hui* (Fashions and Manners of Today), 1913; plate 5, 'The Bath'.

Opposite Charles Martin, *Modes et Manières d'Aujourd'hui* (Fashions and Manners of Today), 1913; plate 2, 'The Snow'.

Opposite Charles Martin, *Modes et Manières d'Aujourd'hui* (Fashions and Manners of Today), 1913; plate 10, 'The Storm'.

Below, left Charles Martin, *Modes et Manières d'Aujourd'hui* (Fashions and Manners of Today), 1913; plate 9, 'The Bridge'.

Below, right Charles Martin, *Modes et Manières d'Aujourd'hui* (Fashions and Manners of Today), 1913; plate 11, 'The Cherries'.

G. BARBIER 1914

La Belle Matineuse

Je t'ai connue à ton matin, ô belle Matineuse! Souviens-toi.....

G. BARBIER 1914

The 1914 issue of *Modes et Manières d'Aujourd'hui*, illustrated by George Barbier, opens with beauties in various stages of undress. Barbier's celebration of the feminine form is seductive though not overtly sexual. In fact, nudity in fashion plates already had a long history when Barbier created these images. 18th-century plates, in common with fashionable portraits of the period,

sometimes depict a woman's exposed breast slipping out of a fashionably low-cut bodice, as illustrated here. Although considered coquettish, a bit of flesh glimpsed in this way was not deemed vulgar or distasteful by 18th-century moral standards, nor was it in this context.

Opposite George Barbier, *Modes et Manières d'Aujourd'hui* (Fashions and Manners of Today), 1914; plate 1, 'The Beautiful Morning Girl'.

Above George Barbier, *Modes et Manières d'Aujourd'hui* (Fashions and Manners of Today), 1914; plate 2, 'The Basin'.

G.BARBIER 1914

L'Oiseau volage

J'avais un perroquet bleu dont j'etais folle.....

Le Coup de vent

Comme il faisait le plus beau temps du monde et que le soleil brillait au ciel printanier.....

Above George Barbier, *Modes et Manières d'Aujourd'hui* (Fashions and Manners of Today), 1914; plate 4, 'The Gust of Wind'.

Opposite George Barbier, *Modes et Manières d'Aujourd'hui* (Fashions and Manners of Today), 1914; plate 3, 'The Flighty Bird'.

GEORGE BARBIER 1914

L'Ilot

Que cet îlot de corail est petit au milieu de cette mer immense et bleue !....

Opposite George Barbier, *Modes et Manières d'Aujourd'hui* (Fashions and Manners of Today), 1914; plate 7, 'The Islet'.

Above George Barbier, *Modes et Manières d'Aujourd'hui* (Fashions and Manners of Today), 1914; plate 5, 'The Red Bow'.

G. BARBIER 1914

Roses dans la nuit
Je ne sais pourquoi j'ai songé, ce soir, à un bouquet d'autrefois.....

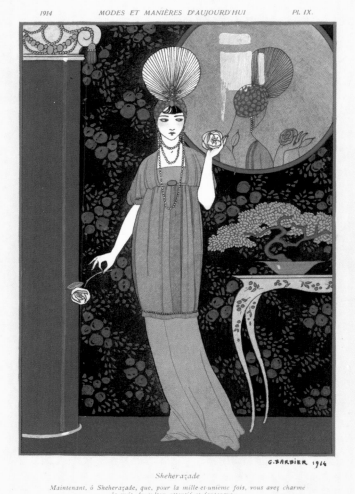

G. BARBIER 1914

Sheherazade
Maintenant, ô Sheherazade, que, pour la mille et unième fois, vous avez charmé
la nuit du sultan attentif et fantasque.....

Opposite George Barbier, *Modes et Manières d'Aujourd'hui* (Fashions and Manners of Today), 1914; plate 11, 'The Dance'.

Left George Barbier, *Modes et Manières d'Aujourd'hui* (Fashions and Manners of Today), 1914; plate 8, 'Roses in the Night'.

Below George Barbier, *Modes et Manières d'Aujourd'hui* (Fashions and Manners of Today), 1914; plate 9, 'Scheherazade'.

Overleaf (left) Georges Lepape, *Modes et Manières d'Aujourd'hui* (Fashions and Manners of Today), 1921; plate 3, 'On Leave'.

Georges Lepape was selected a second time to illustrate the *Modes et Manières d'Aujourd'hui* album dated 1912–19. The album, which was not published until 1921, centred thematically on the years of World War I. While the pursuit of fashion was not the foremost concern for many women during the war, the question of what to wear was indeed a dilemma. Women felt compelled to tone down their dress in recognition of the difficult times, but at the same time they realized that their feminine charms might be a source of pleasure for soldiers home

on leave or recuperating from wounds sustained at the Front. A special version of *Gazette du Bon Ton* produced during the war articulated the sentiments of French women: '"We should appear before sick men as fine as we can", say the women, and they are quite right, for, just as we bring flowers to their bedside, so our presence should form a contrast with the cheerless severity of the hospital ward' (Panama Pacific International Exposition, *The 1915 Mode as Shown by Paris: Panama Pacific International Exposition* (1915), 36).

Overleaf (right) Georges Lepape, *Modes et Manières d'Aujourd'hui* (Fashions and Manners of Today), 1921; plate 13, 'Victory'.

G. BARBIER 1914

La Danse

Je suis beau. Mon corps maigre que vêt une ample robe d'or s'incruste
dans le panneau de laque noir.....

PERMISSIONNAIRE

LA VICTOIRE

Stylizing 'La Femme'

Previous pages André Édouard Marty, *Modes et Manières d'Aujourd'hui* (Fashions and Manners of Today), 1919; plate 1, 'Demobilization'.

The theme of a soldier returning to his family after World War I was close to André Édouard Marty's heart, as he was himself wounded during his service in the war. This illustration accompanies a poem entitled 'La Demobilization' by Tristan Bernard, printed on page 4 of this issue of *Modes et Manières*:

After the horrors of the war,

There was the sweetness of the return.

Take your ease, beautiful soldier,

But your rest will only be one day.

You recover, after your good companion in arms,

Your companion in peace, who wants, in the pleasure, to forget the hard memory,

The memory of the alarms.

Opposite (top) André Édouard Marty, *Modes et Manières d'Aujourd'hui* (Fashions and Manners of Today), 1919; plate 4, 'The Cinema'.

While Thomas Edison is widely credited with inventing the motion-picture camera as early as 1891, the technology behind filmmaking remained largely experimental for several decades. By the 1920s full-length feature films had become commercially viable, and the film industry built lavish 'picture palaces' dedicated to cinematic entertainment. The fame of film stars, such as Charlie Chaplin (seen on the screen here), soon eclipsed that of their theatrical counterparts, who had been the 'It' celebrities of previous generations.

Opposite (bottom) André Édouard Marty, *Modes et Manières d'Aujourd'hui* (Fashions and Manners of Today), 1919; plate 11, 'At the Antiques Shop'.

Above André Édouard Marty, *Modes et Manières d'Aujourd'hui* (Fashions and Manners of Today), 1919; plate 12, 'Wings in the Wind'.

The drab outer and vivid, opulent inner of this cape recalls *iki* fashion of Edo period Japan (1615–1868). Strict sumptuary laws imposed by the ruling Japanese class forbade cash-rich merchants from displaying their wealth with the bright, richly brocaded kimonos that demonstrated wealth and social status. Instead, they redefined chic by adopting muted, unremarkable fabrics lined with costly hand-painted or embroidered silks that were discreetly shown in the course of gesture or movement.

LA MARSEILLAISE

LE GOLF

LA ROBE D'AMOUR

Opposite Robert Bonfils, *Modes et Manières d'Aujourd'hui* (Fashions and Manners of Today), 1920; plate 8, 'The Marseillaise'.

Above, left Robert Bonfils, *Modes et Manières d'Aujourd'hui* (Fashions and Manners of Today), 1920; plate 3, 'Golf'.

The illustrator Robert Bonfils was strongly influenced by the Cubism and Futurism movements in art, and frequently depicted speed and movement in his fashion plates. This image of a woman playing golf is exceptionally dynamic and speaks to the growing number of women who engaged in sports in the 1920s. Sportswear, for which this created a newly burgeoning

market, became an increasingly important category of dress in the 20th century. The image of the fashionable sportswoman was immortalized by F. Scott Fitzgerald in his novel *The Great Gatsby* of 1925, through one of its main female characters, Jordan Baker – a professional golfer.

Above, right Robert Bonfils, *Modes et Manières d'Aujourd'hui* (Fashions and Manners of Today), 1920; plate 1, 'The Love Dress'.

Lingerie intended to heighten amorous pleasure was not part of the arsenal of the 'lady' until the English couturière Lucile began creating 'underclothes as delicate as cobwebs and as beautifully tinted as flowers,

and half the women in London flocked to see them, though [they] had not the courage to buy them at first' (Lucile, Lady Duff-Gordon, *Discretions and Indiscretions*, 1932, 41–42). Despite the fashion for a tightly corseted waist, underclothes of the late Victorian era were more or less utilitarian. Lucile changed the course of the 'unmentionable' industry's history when she created in her couture house a special salon, the Rose Room, which specialized in pleasing the gaze of husbands and lovers with lingerie designed to be as beautiful and sensuous as her other creations.

LE BAIN

CHAPEAUX DE PRINTEMPS

EN ÉCOUTANT SATIE

Above, left Robert Bonfils, *Modes et Manières d'Aujourd'hui* (Fashions and Manners of Today), 1920; plate 5, 'The Bath'.

Above, right Robert Bonfils, *Modes et Manières d'Aujourd'hui* (Fashions and Manners of Today), 1920; plate 7, 'Spring Hats'.

Right Robert Bonfils, *Modes et Manières d'Aujourd'hui* (Fashions and Manners of Today), 1920; plate 11, 'Listening to Satie'.

Guests at this party are enjoying the music of the composer Erik Satie, whose avant-garde compositions were noted for their novel chords and tonal structures. The irreverence and wit of his work is attributed to his affiliation with the artistic movements of Surrealism and Dada. Indeed, the term 'Surrealism' was first used in the programme for Satie's ballet *Parade* (1917), which was costumed by Pablo Picasso and featured sets designed by Jean Cocteau.

Opposite Robert Bonfils, *Modes et Manières d'Aujourd'hui* (Fashions and Manners of Today), 1920; plate 10, 'Towards the Dancing'.

The excess and hedonism of the Jazz Age are elegantly captured in the decadence of these two coats worn for a night out dancing. A period of revelry immediately followed the end of World War I; in the words of F. Scott Fitzgerald in his article 'Echoes of the Jazz Age' in November 1931, 'Scarcely had the staider citizens of the republic caught their breaths when the wildest of all generations, the generation which had been adolescent during the confusion of the War, brusquely shouldered my contemporaries out of the way and danced into the limelight' (*Scribner's Magazine*, XC/5, 460).

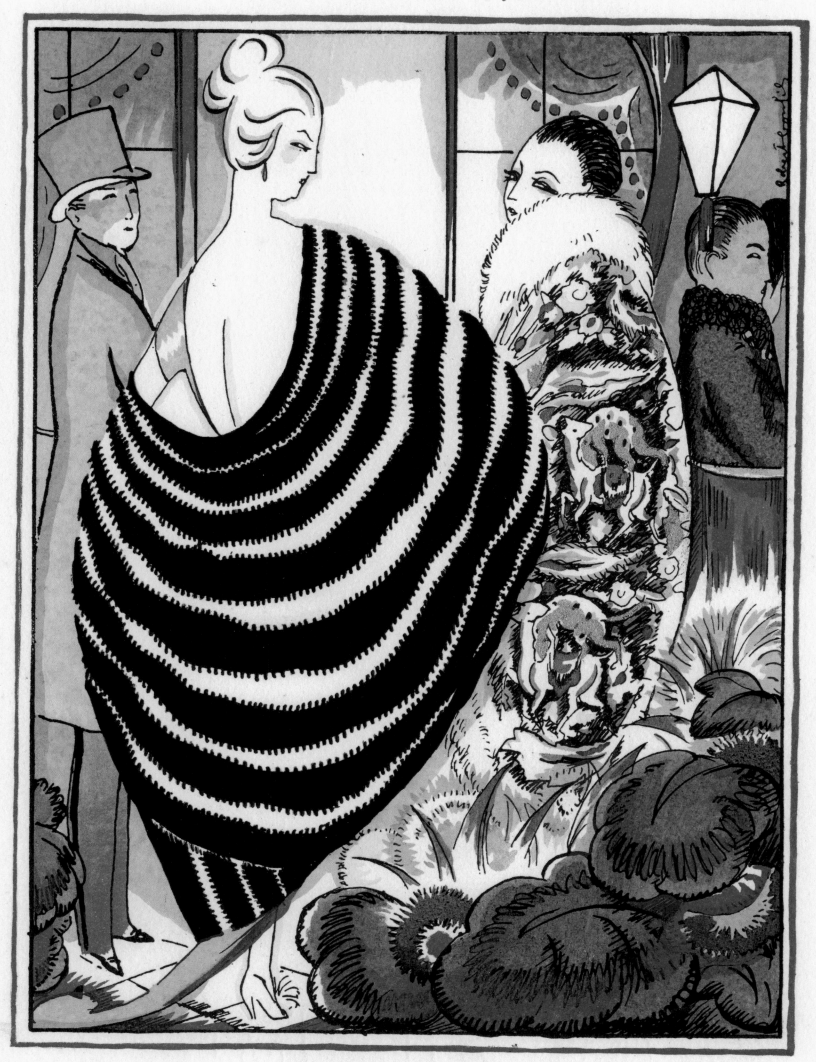

VERS LE DANCING

AMAZONE

BRIC-A-BRAC

Above, left Fernand Siméon, *Modes et Manières d'Aujourd'hui* (Fashions and Manners of Today), 1922; plate 4, 'Amazone'.

An article in *Vogue* on 1 February 1922, 'Good Form on Horseback', accurately describes the riding habit illustrated here, describing it as appropriate for the show ring: 'The Shadbelly coat is quite the oldest hunting-coat ever worn. It resembles a man's dress-coat. . .With this coat can be worn a snow-white stock or a shirt resembling a man's pleated dress-shirt with a high collar and Ascot or a small bow tie. White gloves are always used with this costume and a boutonnière of gardenias or violets. Nothing but a top-hat should ever be worn with a Shadbelly coat. Any other hat is exceedingly in bad form. Patent leather boots and a spur, well put on, complete the picture'. The tan colouring of the coat was probably a matter of artistic licence, in keeping with Fernand Siméon's limited colour palette, since *Vogue* described the Shadbelly coat as 'black or very dark blue'.

Above, right Fernand Siméon, *Modes et Manières d'Aujourd'hui* (Fashions and Manners of Today), 1922; plate 11, 'Bric-a-Brac'.

Opposite Fernand Siméon, *Modes et Manières d'Aujourd'hui* (Fashions and Manners of Today), 1922; plate 10, 'The Attack'.

AUX COURSES

LA PARURE

Above, left Fernand Siméon, *Modes et Manières d'Aujourd'hui* (Fashions and Manners of Today), 1922; plate 5, 'At the Races'.

Above, right Fernand Siméon, *Modes et Manières d'Aujourd'hui* (Fashions and Manners of Today), 1922; plate 9, 'The Dress'.

The column glimpsed out of the window situates this couture house in Paris's place Vendôme, at the end of the fashionable rue de la Paix. A mannequin shows off a new design to potential buyers. Fashion shows with hundreds of guests were a new phenomenon in the early 20th century, and many couture houses continued the traditional practice of showing their clothes to individual buyers in more intimate settings.

Opposite Fernand Siméon, *Modes et Manières d'Aujourd'hui* (Fashions and Manners of Today), 1922; plate 13, 'The Screen'.

OPULENCE RESURRECTED

Journal des Dames et des Modes

·

Journal of Ladies and Fashions

6

'For the delectation of the elect.'
Alice Friend, 1913[1]

After a seventy-three-year hiatus, the landmark publication *Journal des Dames et des Modes* was reborn in 1912. Publisher Tom Antongini's fashion and society journal was modelled on its late 18th-century predecessor of the same name, which issued the popular fashion-plate series 'Costume Parisien' uninterrupted for more than forty years. The celebrated French writer and journalist Anatole France explained the impetus for the return of the title in the inaugural issue on 1 June 1912:

> *It is reborn by the hand of several ingenious spirits and artists. It is reborn for the connoisseurs (if there are any left) who are not content with fashion journals with subscriptions of several thousand and illustrated with photography. And if the editors are bringing back to us exactly the same, in its format, with its paper, printing, engraving and colour processes, the old classic of former times, they intend to amiably continue the title and for it to become the charming fashion classic of today and tomorrow.[2]*

First issued in 1797 by the Parisian bookseller Jean-Baptiste Sellèque and former priest Pierre de La Mésangère, *Journal des Dames et des Modes* was one of the first French fashion publications to emerge in the wake of the French Revolution. From its debut, it set a standard of elegance and sophistication for ladies' magazines, a segment of the publishing industry that saw explosive growth during the 19th century. The publication was considered an authoritative source on Parisian culture, society and fashion, and every five days, it issued the latest word on dress, art, theatre, literature, music, philosophy and education. 'We have already remarked that fashion decides everything in France,' wrote *Journal* in 1813, 'the manner in which we dress, the style in which we dance, the particular type of music, and more or less the success of dramatic and literary debuts; everything is determined by fashion.'[3]

The little journal, sometimes known affectionately as *La Mésangère*, had a strong international following (subscriptions were delivered as far away as Russia, Spain and Turkey) that centred on the highly desirable nature of its exquisite, hand-tinted 'Costume Parisien' fashion plates.[4] The plates were produced by some of the leading illustrators of the day, including Philibert-Louis Debucourt and the father-son artist duo Carle and Horace Vernet. *Journal* was so beloved during the 19th century that it was sometimes faked and sold on the street by unscrupulous printers looking for a quick way to make cash.[5] It left an indelible imprint on the future of fashion journalism; upon its relaunch in 1912, American *Vogue* ran not one but two articles on the collectible nature of the early years of the title, one of which noted: 'It is said that there is but one complete collection of La Méssangère's [*sic*] *Le Journal des Dames et des Modes* in existence, and for this its owner has refused 30,000 francs.'[6] Today, the original run of 'Costume Parisien' serves as one of the most important records of fashion during the Directoire and Empire periods of the early 19th century.

The publisher Tom Antongini reinvented *Journal* through the lens of modernity, deliberately positioning it as the artistic, luxurious alternative to the mass-produced magazines of the day, such as *Les Modes* and *Femina*. Hoping to capitalize on the title's former renown and cachet, he stuck close to the format established by his predecessor. The

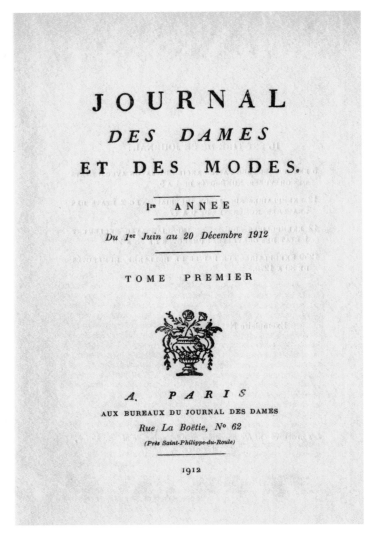

small, unbound journal was comprised of just eight pages of text. The cover was similarly of utilitarian blue-grey paper, simply printed with the title centred inside a demure floral border; the fashion plates mirrored the original run of 'Costume Parisien', right down to the placement of the title, the sequential numbering and the descriptive text. The hand-tinting method previously used to colour the plates was replaced by pochoir, which had become très chic following the acclaimed publication of *Les Robes de Paul Poiret racontées par Paul Iribe* (1908) and *Les Choses de Paul Poiret vues par Georges Lepape* (1911).

Where Iribe and Lepape's fashion illustrations for the luxury albums by Poiret, and also Jeanne Paquin, were given an artistic pretext as a way to lend legitimacy to the medium, the pages of Antongini's *Journal* overtly celebrated the association of art and fashion. Overwhelmingly, the garments shown in its 'Costume Parisien' plates lived only on the page – fictional creations born in the imagination of the illustrator – as opposed to those in rival publications, such as *Gazette du Bon Ton* (first published in November 1912), which interspersed designs by artists and couturiers. As a tri-monthly publication, *Journal*, perhaps more so than the pioneering couturier albums, was instrumental in establishing fashion illustration as a valid medium for fine and classically trained artists seeking alternative forms of

income. Over the course of its run, more than two dozen artists contributed plates, including Léon Bakst, George Barbier, Umberto Brunelleschi, Bernard Boutet de Monvel, Étienne Drian, Charles Martin and Gerda Wegener. All were instrumental in defining the look of the Art Moderne era, as their work in *Journal* brought them to the attention of a broader audience, garnering them commissions outside the realm of fashion. Soon their avant-garde aesthetic seeped into all forms of cultural production: fashion, publishing, theatre, film and advertising.

Antongini cultivated an elite readership by limiting his edition of *Journal* to only 1,279 copies in total; 1,250 standard issues as well as 29 deluxe issues, which were printed on premium paper and included additional sets of 'Costume Parisien'. In 1912 a subscription cost between 100 and 500 francs.[7] At this deliberately exclusive price, it is no surprise that the contents of each issue catered to those living a lifestyle of luxury and leisure. The advertisements are especially telling of the elements considered essential for an elegant life: those for Louis Vuitton luggage and Guerlain cosmetics appear next to countless offerings for resorts and spas, while early commercial airlines publicize their passenger routes between London and Paris. The crème de la crème of Parisian society was covered by *Journal*; the latest Persian ball given by Madame so-and-so was only

Chapeau attaché avec un fichu. Redingote de Levantine.

Above Journal des Dames et des Modes (Journal of Ladies and Fashions), 1811; 'Parisian Costume: Hat Secured with a *Fichu*; Levantine Riding Coat'.

Opposite, left Journal des Dames et des Modes (Journal of Ladies and Fashions); cover.

Opposite, right Journal des Dames et des Modes (Journal of Ladies and Fashions), 1912; title page.

to be eclipsed in the next issue by the subsequent Oriental fancy-dress fete given by another socially prominent hostess. The issue of 20 August 1912 declared: 'Without doubt, the Persian ball is *over*. . .we cannot ever revere the folly of the eccentricity of forms, the colours, the hairstyles that were undertaken in the name of art.'[8] Yet a mere ten days earlier, an article had appeared within its pages lauding the erudition of the current Orientalist vogue.[9] One would be wise to consider the witty and undeniably delightful prose of *Journal* with a certain measure of sarcastic scepticism, as the prevailing winds of fashion were known to change frequently, and without any warning.

Sadly, the run of Antongini's *Journal des Dames et des Modes* was to last just over two years. The final issue was dated 1 August 1914; Germany declared war on France only three days later, and the publication, which had been born as a result of fortunes determined at the end of the French Revolution, had oddly come full circle, to be extinguished by the outbreak of World War I.[10] However, the Paris of these years shines brightly within its pages. In the words of Antongini:

> *The Paris of 1913 and '14, for those who remember it clearly, was a city in which refinement, elegance, joie de vivre, and insouciance had reached an unsurpassable height. Everyone, it seemed, lived only for pleasure, and the most unexpected and unheard-of material and intellectual pleasures came the way of individuals of every social class with such facility as to make one think that the Golden Age was about to return. Perhaps Fate, knowing that the greatest war the world had ever seen was to break out in a few months, thus granted thousands of doomed souls this final consolation in advance.*[11]

1. Margaret Alice Friend, 'Fashion: After the Manner of an Old Style-Book', *Vogue*, 15 February 1913, 31.
2. Anatole France, 'Paris', *Journal des Dames et des Modes*, 1 June 1912, 2.
3. Annemarie Kleinert, *Le Journal des Dames et des Modes: Ou la Conquête de l'Europe Féminine (1797–1839)* (Stuttgart, 2001), 6.
4. *Ibid.*, 3.
5. *Ibid.*, 9.
6. 'Fashion', 106.
7. This sum can be contextualized by one of the advertisements that appeared repeatedly in the pages of *Journal*: a Parisian car dealer offered its entry-level vehicle for 1,500 francs, a mere three times the price of a super-deluxe subscription to *Journal des Dames et des Modes*.
8. *Journal des Dames et des Modes*, 20 August 1913, 1.

9. Whereas the original run of *Journal* was issued every five days, Antongini's appeared every ten days, on the first, tenth and twentieth of each month.
10. The very existence of the magazine was entwined with the period's tumultuous political events, which had dealt a curious hand to each of the journal's two founders. Until 1793, Mésangère had been a member of the Congrégation des Pères de la Doctrine Chrétienne and a professor at the prestigious college La Flèche. During the Reign of Terror, however, many religious orders and universities were disbanded, and thirty-two-year-old Mésangère soon found himself in search of a new vocation. It is not clear how the two entrepreneurs first met, but three years into their partnership, Sellèque was killed as the result of a failed attempt to assassinate Napoleon Bonaparte.
11. Quoted in F. M. Ricci, *Costumes Parisiens: Journal des Dames et des Modes* (Paris, 1979), 1.

Top row, left George Barbier, *Journal des Dames et des Modes* (Journal of Ladies and Fashions), 1912; 'Pearl-grey satin tailored suit. Black straw hat'.

Top row, centre Umberto Brunelleschi, *Journal des Dames et des Modes* (Journal of Ladies and Fashions), 1912; 'Promenade dress in checked surah and hand-painted taffeta, lined with black velvet. Straw hat with a swandown panache'.

Top row, right Armand Vallée, *Journal des Dames et des Modes* (Journal of Ladies and Fashions), 1912; 'Young girls' dresses: one in white seersucker and orange taffeta; the other in embroidered white wool'.

Bottom row, left Charles Martin, *Journal des Dames et des Modes* (Journal of Ladies and Fashions), 1912; 'White seersucker sheath, embroidered and painted. Emerald-coloured velvet blouse with brocaded poppies. Pearl belt'.

Bottom row, centre Fernand Siméon, *Journal des Dames et des Modes* (Journal of Ladies and Fashions), 1912; 'Auburn-and-black velvet jacket on a painted "frissonnette" sheath. Velvet hat with aigrette'.

Bottom row, right Suzanne Sesboüé, *Journal des Dames et des Modes* (Journal of Ladies and Fashions), 1912; 'Girl's dress in blue velvet decorated with skunk fur. White suede gaiters'.

Opposite Armand Vallée, *Journal des Dames et des Modes* (Journal of Ladies and Fashions), 1913; 'Full dress'.

The toilette of a fashionable woman is never complete without accessories, and during the early 20th century entire sets, or *parure*, of fine jewelry often included matching fans. The beauty featured here has coordinated her rings, necklace and bracelets with a fan ornamented with precious metals and jewels.

Grande Parure

Petit loden Tailleur en laine d'Ecosse. Grosses bottines lacées

Opposite Marie-Madeleine Franc-Nohain, *Journal des Dames et des Modes* (Journal of Ladies and Fashions), 1913; 'Grey-green-wool morning tailored suit; yellow-and-grey taffeta belt, facing and collar'.

Above Maurice Taquoy, *Journal des Dames et des Modes* (Journal of Ladies and Fashions), 1913; 'Small Scottish-wool loden suit, large laced-up ankle boots'.

Dioné dessin de Bakst réalisé par Paquin.

Robe de taffetas à fleurs et ottoman de soie. Chapeau de tulle.

Above, left Léon Bakst, *Journal des Dames et des Modes* (Journal of Ladies and Fashions), 1913; 'Dione – drawing by Bakst and costume realized by Paquin'.

Theatre was a mainstay of early 20th-century popular entertainment, and the costumes from particularly popular productions sometimes influenced the fashion of the period. Léon Bakst, designer for the avant-garde Russian dance company the Ballets Russes, created the ensemble shown here. In the wake of the distinction he garnered for his sets and costumes, Bakst turned his hand and eye towards women's fashion, partnering in 1913 with the couturière Jeanne Paquin, who executed his designs. The collaboration was lauded by *Vogue* in an article entitled 'Fashion: The Bakst-Paquin Combination' on 15 June 1913: 'The elaborate designs of Bakst were carried out even to the most minute detail, and this produced a collection of dresses which, in every respect, gives the impression of "jamais vu." Monsieur Bakst and Madame Paquin are to be congratulated on the result. The artist has shown us another aspect of his remarkable talent, and the Maison Paquin will never regret having thrown open its doors to this artist.'

Above, right Loeze, *Journal des Dames et des Modes* (Journal of Ladies and Fashions), 1913; 'Dress in flower-patterned taffeta and silk ottoman. Tulle hat'.

Opposite Marie-Madeleine Franc-Nohain, *Journal des Dames et des Modes* (Journal of Ladies and Fashions), 1913; 'Yellow-and-white polka-dot seersucker dress. Little girl's dress in green and dark red tartan'.

The precise and dainty style of Marie-Madeleine Franc-Nohain – who signed her works 'mfn' – is distinctive among illustrators of the period. The fashion plates she created for magazines frequently depicted tender moments of maternal doting. It must have been natural for her to include children in her works, since she was an author and illustrator of children's books – the field for which she is best known. Along with a handful of other female illustrators, including Gerda Wegener and Valentine Gross, she was respected in a field traditionally dominated by men. She contributed to the French satirical journal *Le Rire*, which employed the crème de la crème of Paris illustrators, including Paul Iribe and Henri de Toulouse-Lautrec.

Robe de crépon blanc à pois jaune. — Robe de fillette
en écossais cerise et vert.

Toilette aux couleurs gagnantes

*Manteau de voyage à pèlerine. Bleu ancien
Robe de taffetas noire*

*Petite robe de jardin, par Poiret, en crêpe de laine bleu.
Fichu et poignets de lingerie*

Above, left Jan van Brock, *Journal des Dames et des Modes* (Journal of Ladies and Fashions), 1913; 'Outfit in winning colours'.

In the early 20th century, attending the horse races was a popular pastime and a highly anticipated social event. The confines of the stands and paddock created a captive audience for sartorial display. Society women and professional models and actresses hired to show off the couturiers' latest creations preened before photographers, who came to document the best-dressed women in Paris. This association of the modelling of clothes with the racetrack meant that professional models of the time were sometimes referred to as 'jockeys'.

Above, right Marie-Madeleine Franc-Nohain, *Journal des Dames et des Modes* (Journal of Ladies and Fashions), 1913; 'Ancient-blue travelling coat with cape. Black taffeta dress'.

Left Charles Martin, *Journal des Dames et des Modes* (Journal of Ladies and Fashions), 1913; 'Little garden dress, by Poiret, in blue wool crêpe. Lingerie scarf and cuffs'.

Opposite Drian, *Journal des Dames et des Modes* (Journal of Ladies and Fashions), 1913; 'Pastel-pink charmeuse coat lined with white fox'.

Manteau de charmeuse rose pastel garni de renard blanc.

Right Jan van Brock, *Journal des Dames et des Modes* (Journal of Ladies and Fashions), 1913; 'Leopard-lined topaz satin dress, with matching leopard muff'.

Below Honoré, *Journal des Dames et des Modes* (Journal of Ladies and Fashions), 1913; 'Embroidered blue-duvetyn dress, lined with otter skin'.

Opposite Pierre Legrain, *Journal des Dames et des Modes* (Journal of Ladies and Fashions), 1913; 'Maize-coloured velvet dress. Short velvet jacket lined with miniver fur'.

The boldly striped wallpaper seen in this plate bears a striking resemblance to the wallpaper in an undated sketch for a drawing room by the interior-design firm Martine. In 1911 Paul Poiret expanded his operations beyond his couture house, launching a perfume company called Rosine as well as Martine, which was comprised of three entities: École Martine,

1913 Costumes Parisiens *110*

*Robe de Satin topaxe garnie de Léopard
Manchon auffi de Léopard*

1913 Costumes Parisiens *115*

*Robe de duvetin bleu vitrail brodée au point lancé
et garnie de loutre.*

Atelier Martine and Maison Martine. École Martine was an experimental art school for young, working-class girls, run by Poiret with the assistance of his friend and collaborator Raoul Dufy. Poiret did not instruct or criticize the girls' work, but rather gave them free rein to interpret nature unimpeded by 'the false and empirical precepts they had received at school'. The Martine students' instinctive designs were translated into wallpaper, rugs, textiles, hand-painted glassware and other home furnishings by Atelier Martine, and sold through Maison Martine boutiques across Europe and in high-end department stores in the United States.

Robe de velours maïs.
Petite veste de velours noir bordée de vair.

Une Amazone

1913 Costumes Parisiens 128

Robe de charmeuse garnie de zibeline et d'hermine
Gilet d'hermine—Souliers clergyman

Above Victor Lhuer, *Journal des Dames et des Modes* (Journal of Ladies and Fashions), 1913; 'Charmeuse dress lined with sable and ermine fur. Ermine waistcoat. "Clergyman" shoes'.

Muffs made from exotic fur were fashionable accessories for hundreds of years. During the 17th and 18th centuries, both men and women used muffs not only to protect their hands from the cold, but also for storing small personal items. Some women even used them to carry small toy dogs. By the early 20th century, however, muffs were a largely feminine accessory, and those made from ermine, sable, moleskin and fox were favoured. Price tags for fine muffs could be astronomical; in 1912 the disappearance of a wealthy American woman's $15,000 muff while she was abroad in London was reported by the *New York Times*.

Right George Barbier, *Journal des Dames et des Modes* (Journal of Ladies and Fashions), 1913; '"Old-style" taffeta short cape lined with green chenille. Muff embroidered with pearls'.

Opposite Bernard Boutet de Monvel, *Journal des Dames et des Modes* (Journal of Ladies and Fashions), 1913; 'An Amazon'.

The riding habit, one of the few specialized pieces of sportswear in women's wardrobes for centuries, has traditionally taken its styling cues – in terms of tailoring, fabric and colour palette – from menswear. By the early 20th century, knowledge of the proper riding attire for various situations had evolved into a form of etiquette. Fashion magazines such as *Vogue* identified at least four separate occasions for which fashionable equestrian dress could be worn – country riding, in-town or bridle-path riding, the show ring and the formal hunt – all of which called for specific silhouettes and accessories.

1913 Costumes Parisiens 116

1913 G. BARBIER

Mantelet de taffetas "à la vieille" garni d'une
chenille verte.—Manchon brodé de perles

Toilette d'après-midi

Robe de satin pékiné à volants de nansouk

Manteau du soir en velours frappé garni de soie brochée d'argent

Above, left Armand Vallée, *Journal des Dames et des Modes* (Journal of Ladies and Fashions), 1914; 'Afternoon outfit'.

In their autobiographies, both Paul Poiret and Lucile claim responsibility for launching the ultra-trim skirt silhouette, or 'hobble skirt', seen here. The opening at the bottom of the skirt was so narrow that it prevented a woman from taking a full stride. Although quite popular, the style was ridiculed widely for its sheer impracticality. Many years later, Lucile reminisced in her memoir *A Woman of Temperament*: 'The Suffragettes were screaming for freedom in Trafalgar Square while I launched in Paris the silliest, most helpless, most irresponsible fashion that women have ever submitted to. . .Society tottered through the last of the pre-War parties, waved tiny lace handkerchiefs and carried elaborate parasols until the War came with its sweeping changes.'

Above, right André Stefan, *Journal des Dames et des Modes* (Journal of Ladies and Fashions), 1914; 'Satin dress with nainsook flounces'.

Left Unsigned, 1914 ('Evening coat in crushed velvet lined with silver-embroidered silk').

Opposite Armand Vallée, *Journal des Dames et des Modes* (Journal of Ladies and Fashions), 1914; 'Visiting outfits: one red ottoman with military-style braiding of silk and silver bells, the other of faille with large ribs'.

Toilettes de visite, l'une d'ottoman rouge à brandebourgs de soie et grelots d'argent, l'autre de faille à grosses côtes.

*Manteau d'après-midi en duvetyn citron,
avec une boucle de moire*

Robe de serge bleue à volant écossais.

Opposite Unsigned, *Journal des Dames et des Modes* (Journal of Ladies and Fashions), 1914; 'Afternoon coat in lemon-coloured duvetyn with a moiré buckle'.

Above Jan van Brock, *Journal des dames et des modes* (Journal of Ladies and Fashions), 1914; 'Blue twill dress with tartan flounces'.

The silhouette seen here, which pairs a long, narrow, tubular skirt with a shorter, flared overskirt, is often called the 'lampshade' or 'minaret' tunic. The style was launched by Poiret, who created a costume of similar shape for his wife, Denise, to wear to his famous 1,002nd Night Party in 1911.

In 1913 he revived the silhouette, this time in costumes for the successful play *Le Minaret*, and he subsequently offered a modified adaptation of the 'minaret' tunic to his couture clientele in his Autumn 1913 collection – but he was not alone. 'The tunic is omnipresent at every house', remarked the *New York Times* on 14 September 1913. The tunic, often sheer, remained a pervasive element of fashion in 1914, and was the direct predecessor of the silhouette that dominated just before the outbreak of the war: a long, wide skirt paired with a narrow-hemmed underskirt (see pages 133 and 137).

Robe de Garden Party en mousseline blanche et liberty orange

Above Robert Dammy, *Journal des Dames et des Modes* (Journal of Ladies and Fashions), 1914; 'Garden-party dress in white muslin and orange liberty'.

Opposite Gerda Wegener, *Journal des Dames et des Modes* (Journal of Ladies and Fashions), 1914; 'Gaberdine dress with hand-embroidered flounces'.

The fact that the Danish Gerda Wegener was one of the few female artists to find commercial success in Paris during the 1910s and 1920s is perhaps one of the least intriguing aspects of her extraordinary life. As well as producing illustrations for fashion publications, she also illustrated several volumes of erotica. Wegener's willingness to explore themes of love, mystery and sex were undoubtedly inspired by her relationship with her husband, the painter Einar Wegener. She often photographed and painted her husband as his feminine alter ego Lili Elbe, and in 1930 'Lili' became the first recorded person in history to undergo gender-reassignment surgery.

Cop. J. N. Ab et C.ie 1914

Veste de soie écossaise. Jupe de crépon de coton souris.

Jupe de grosse toile.

Robe à retroussis

*Veste de drap fin sur jupe de même
à tunique de taffetas pékiné*

Above, left Gerda Wegener, *Journal des Dames et des Modes*
(Journal of Ladies and Fashions), 1914; 'Coarse-linen skirt'.

Above, right Gerda Wegener, *Journal des Dames et des Modes*
(Journal of Ladies and Fashions), 1914; 'Lapel dress'.

Left Victor Lhuer, *Journal des Dames et des Modes* (Journal
of Ladies and Fashions), 1914; 'Fine-cotton jacket on a skirt
of the same fabric with a taffeta tunic'.

Opposite Gerda Wegener, *Journal des Dames et des Modes*
(Journal of Ladies and Fashions), 1914; 'Tartan silk jacket.
Mouse-grey seersucker dress'.

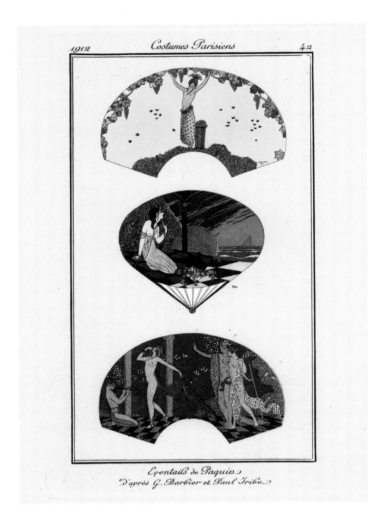

Eventails de Paquin
D'après G. Barbier et Paul Iribe.

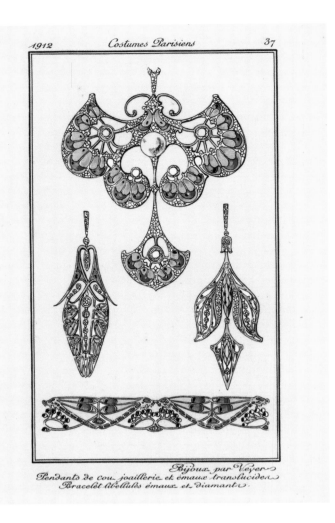

Bijoux, par Vever
Pendants de cou, joaillerie et émaux translucides
Bracelet libellules émaux et diamant.

Chapeaux par Arlette Carus: 1, en taffetas bleu et gancé garni fleurs; 2, en liseré garni satin noir et perruche; 3, en satin noir garni de numidie; 4, en satin blanc garni fantaisie pintade argentée; 5, en satin noir et blanc garni fantaisie crosse; 6, en liseré garni couteaux; 7, en satin noir garni fantaisie crosse et aigrette.

Above, left Unsigned, *Journal des Dames et des Modes* (Journal of Ladies and Fashions), 1914; 'Fans from the house of Paquin based on the creations of G. Barbier and Paul Iribe'.

Above, right Unsigned, *Journal des Dames et des Modes* (Journal of Ladies and Fashions), 1914; 'Jewelry by Vever'.

Left Unsigned, *Journal des Dames et des Modes* (Journal of Ladies and Fashions), 1914; 'Hats by Arlette Carus'.

The hat with an all-round rolling brim was one of the hardest shapes to create, demanding the 'skill of a genius'. The sculpting and moulding of crowns and brims was only one technique involved in the creation of a hat. The feathers, which were an essential element of millinery during the 1910s, were frequently dyed and then pressed, as *Vogue* noted on 1 September 1912, 'into new and unnatural shapes such as a question mark and the "setter's tail."'

Opposite George Barbier, *Journal des Dames et des Modes* (Journal of Ladies and Fashions), 1914; 'Silver-brocade formal evening dress. Blue wig, aigrettes'.

The blue wig worn by the woman of George Barbier's reverie was, at least in part, rooted in reality. The couturières Lucile and Jeanne Paquin were both known for styling their models in coloured wigs, imparting an air of fantasy to their designs.

Grande robe du soir en brocart d'argent.
Perruque bleue, aigrettes.

Toilette de taffetas imprimé
Chapeau de paille.

GERDA·WEGENER.

Petite robe de taffetas pour l'après-midi.

FABIVS

Robe de taffetas et mousseline de soie peinte.

Above, left Gerda Wegener, *Journal des Dames et des Modes* (Journal of Ladies and Fashions), 1914; 'Little afternoon taffeta dress'.

Above, right Fabius, *Journal des Dames et des Modes* (Journal of Ladies and Fashions), 1914; 'Taffeta and painted-chiffon dress'.

Opposite George Barbier, *Journal des Dames et des Modes* (Journal of Ladies and Fashions), 1914; 'Printed taffeta dress. Straw hat'.

This plate is a beautiful example of the range of techniques employed by pochoir colourists. A delicate blue gradient gives the illusion of sky, and the dappled texture of the grass is achieved by tamping a pompom brush loaded with green pigment on to the page. The blush caressing this beauty's cheeks was, no doubt, applied freehand.

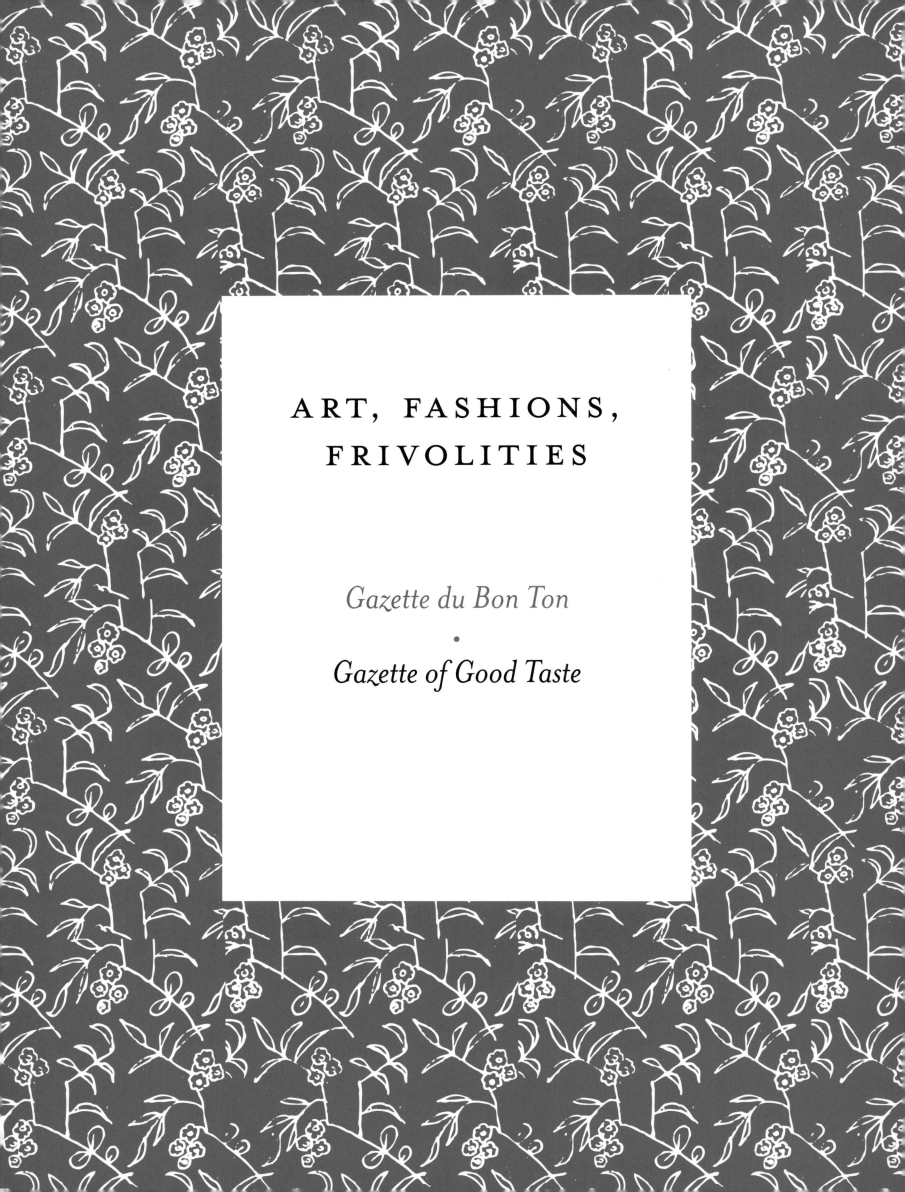

ART, FASHIONS, FRIVOLITIES

Gazette du Bon Ton

·

Gazette of Good Taste

7

'The clothing of a woman is a pleasure for the eye that cannot be judged inferior to the other arts.'
Inaugural issue of *Gazette du Bon Ton*, 1912[1]

The year 1912 was a prolific one for pochoir in fashion illustration. Where the time between 1908 and 1911 had yielded only three such publications (those by Poiret and Paquin), this was more than doubled in 1912 alone. The debuts of *La Mode en mil neuf cent douze chez Marcelle Demay*, *Modes et Manières d'Aujourd'hui* and *Journal des Dames et des Modes* were followed by *Gazette du Bon Ton*, a monthly fashion magazine by the publishing visionary Lucien Vogel. It was launched just five months after *Journal des Dames et des Modes*, in November 1912, but would outlive its rival magazine by thirteen years, running until 1925 – although publication was suspended for six years owing to the events and aftermath of World War I. Like *Journal*, *Gazette* was a loose-leaf publication, printed in a limited run with a high subscription cost, and was intended for an elite readership preoccupied with the art of high living and the cultivation of good taste – the literal translation of its title phrase 'le bon ton'. Its subtitle, 'Art, Fashion and Frivolities', conveyed the light-hearted tone of the magazine; its sense of fun and humour is one of its most endearing qualities.

'When fashion becomes an art,' declared the inaugural issue, 'a fashion magazine must itself become an arts magazine. It will offer, on the one hand, the most recent models to emerge from the ateliers of the rue de la Paix and, on the other hand, in the painters' watercolours, that fashion sense, that charming and bold interpretation that is their hallmark.'[2] Where *Journal* depended largely on stylized, artistic depictions of fashionable dress, Vogel took *Gazette* one step further and signed exclusive contracts with seven

of the leading Parisian couture houses of the day: Poiret, Paquin, Doucet, Dœuillet, Chéruit, Redfern and Worth – and the couturiers' designs featured within the pages of *Gazette* could not be found in any other publication. Each of those seven couturiers was given one pochoir plate per issue to depict the creation of their choice, but its interpretation was left entirely to Vogel's team of illustrators, who were given liberal artistic licence. Three plates in each issue were not couturier creations at all, but rather designs from the artist's imagination. 'The artist has discovered the couturier, and vice versa,' *Vogue* observed in 1914, 'and they find that they were not so very far apart after all; one uses paints as a medium and the other silks and satins.'[3] Indeed, it was Vogel's intention to use *Gazette du Bon Ton* to position fashion as a natural extension of the fine arts.

More than eighty illustrators contributed to *Gazette* over the course of its publication, infusing it with a broad variety of styles that ranged from the stylized realism of Étienne Drian and Pierre Brissaud to the fantastical and theatrical dreamscapes created by Georges Lepape and George Barbier. The scenario depicted in each plate, as well as its witty and often humorous text, was the creation of the illustrator, and captions, such as 'Cursed Wind', 'Be Discreet', and 'The Woman Who Died of Love', complemented the unique vision of each artist. Besides a brief mention of the couturier – if it was a couturier's design and not that of the illustrator – any lengthy description, such as the garment's fabric and cut, was divorced from the plate and tucked away at the back of each issue.[4] The garments portrayed were treated as if they were subjects in a painting, the fashion plates masked as a story-telling picture.

An article of 1914 in American *Vogue* provides a rare, revealing look at the 'school' of young artists at the heart of *Gazette*'s success, dubbing them the 'Beau Brummels [*sic*] of the Brush':

> It is rather, in fact, the certain dandyism of dress and manner which is a constant characteristic of the group that makes them a 'school'. Their hat brims are a wee bit broader than the modish ones of the day. . .their coats are pinched in a little. . .a bracelet slipping down over a wrist at an unexpected moment betrays a love of luxury.[5]

The article is accompanied by paintings and photographs of the dapper gents, the self-proclaimed 'Knights of the Bracelet': Bernard Boutet de Monvel, his cousin Pierre Brissaud, Georges Lepape, George Barbier, Jean Besnard, André Édouard Marty, Charles Martin and Paul Iribe. Not coincidentally, most of the men had received their fine-arts training together at the École des Beaux-Arts, and belonged to the same social circle as Vogel. *Vogue* posited Vogel as the enterprising 'impresario' of the group, who had conceived *Gazette* both as employment for his friends and as a forum for their artistic talent.

The veracity of *Vogue*'s claims aside, Vogel cultivated a diverse range of artistic styles within the pages of *Gazette* that propelled the discourse between art and fashion forward, and further validated fashion and fashion illustration as outlets of modern artistic practice. Art was the centrepiece of the publication – a visually arresting, pervasive element that enticed the reader with the turn of every page. Interspersed with works contributed by leading literary figures of the period are striking, animated characters of the artist's fancy: one of Barbier's sultry sultanas might suggestively insert her sinuous body into the lines of text of one article, while another article's visual companion could be an illustration by Martin that spanned not one but two pages. As important to the spirit of the magazine as its visual artistry were its witty and whimsical articles on topics of interest to high society. The names of the day's cultural innovators, such as Sergei Diaghilev and Léon Bakst of the Ballets Russes, peppered *Gazette*'s pages, alongside coverage of the latest works of renowned composers including Erik Satie. Today, *Gazette* is a captivating source of information on the fashionable, modern *bon vivant* lifestyle of the 1910s and 1920s. Even in its own lifetime, the publication was held in such regard that, in 1920, special compilations of its pre-war issues were marketed as collector's items.

The American publishing mogul and *Vogue* founder Condé Nast was largely responsible for the continued success of *Gazette* after the end of World War I. Nast – who was a great admirer of the publication and a staunch supporter of the French fashions promoted in his own fashion magazines – bought into the magazine and ended its six-year hiatus in 1920. On the eve of *Gazette*'s suspension in 1914, he had collaborated with Vogel to produce a special edition of the magazine, *The 1915 Mode: As Shown by Paris*, which commemorated the exhibition of Parisian fashions at the Panama Pacific International Exposition in San Francisco. The issue was a tribute to France's indomitable spirit in the face of the current war, and a declaration of the country's continued dominance in matters of fashion and taste. 'Paris owed the world this proof of her incorruptible vitality,' the issue proclaimed, 'as immutable when at war as during times of peace.'[6]

In 1922 *Gazette* informed its readers that – following complaints about the magazine's cost, which had soared to 300 francs per year – it was slashing its subscription in half. (The cost of an annual subscription to *Gazette du Bon Ton* had reached the equivalent of the advertised price of a second-hand car.) The use of pochoir became extremely limited, and although not entirely eliminated, the costly, laborious technique was largely replaced by the less expensive, easier method of chromolithography. Despite the decline in its artistic integrity, *Gazette* would continue until 1925, when its sixty-ninth and final issue was released. Today, it is extremely rare to find a full run of *Gazette du Bon Ton*, with all its treasured pochoir plates intact. The fashion plates are often sold as separate entities – standing alone as works of art, as Vogel intended – and collected by connoisseurs of fashion and art alike.

Opposite Gazette du Bon Ton (Gazette of Good Taste), 1912, issue 1; cover, subtitled 'Art – Fashions & Frivolities'.

GAZETTE
DU
BON TON

ART ~ MODES
&
FRIVOLITÉS

Lucien VOGEL · Directeur

Emile LEVY Editeur
LIBRAIRIE CENTRALE DES BEAUX~ARTS
13 Rue Lafayette PARIS

1. *Gazette du Bon Ton*, November 1912, 1.
2. *Ibid.*, 2.
3. 'Beau Brummels [sic] of the Brush', *Vogue*, 15 June 1914, 37.
4. Before the 19th century, the descriptive text found on fashion plates was the primary source of information on the fashionable cut, colour and trimming for women who ordered their wardrobes *couture à façon*. They not only selected the textiles used to created their custom wardrobes, but also guided their dressmakers and tailors in the making of their garments, sometimes down to the very last placement of a specific ribbon or fringe. The trend towards removing this sort of text from the face of the fashion plate can probably be related to the birth of haute couture in the middle of the 19th century, when the roles reversed and couturiers began to guide their clients in matters of taste.
5. 'Beau Brummels of the Brush', 35.
6. Paul Adams, 'La Costume de Paris', *The 1915 Mode: As Shown by Paris* (1915), 8. *The 1915 Mode* was essentially an English translation of *Gazette*'s issue of summer 1915; it featured the same fashion plates but added a selection of fashion photographs of garments seen in the exhibition. This was the only time *Gazette* ever appeared in English; even the version published by Nast in the United States, *Gazette du Bon Genre*, counted on the sophistication of its audience, being published in French and advertised as 'the most beautiful, luxurious, and expensive magazine in the world' (advertisement in *Printer's Ink Monthly*, March 1921, 61).

LA FLEUR ET LE MIROIR

Robe du soir de Chéruit

Above Umberto Brunelleschi, *Gazette du Bon Ton* (Gazette of Good Taste), 1912, issue 2; 'The Flower and the Mirror. Evening Dress by Chéruit'.

Opposite Javier Francisco Gosé, *Gazette du Bon Ton* (Gazette of Good Taste), 1912, issue 1; 'At the Comedy Theatre. Opera Coat by Paquin'.

While the couturière Jeanne Paquin denounced the most extreme elements of the Orientalist trend – such as the *jupes-culottes* – the opera coat in this plate demonstrates that she was not entirely immune to Eastern inspiration. The illustrator Francisco Javier Gosé depicts a Paquin opera coat that incorporates both embroidered and beaded Asian-inspired motifs, while the silhouette of the garment resembles a kimono. An example of this garment from 1912 is held in the Anna Wintour Costume Center at the Metropolitan Museum of Art in New York.

A LA COMÉDIE

Manteau de Théâtre, par Paquin

A CHAMONIX

Costume d'homme et de femme pour les Sports d'hiver

Opposite Paul Méras, *Gazette du Bon Ton* (Gazette of Good Taste), 1912, issue 1; 'The Rendez-Vous in the Park. Full Evening Dress by Worth'.

The prestigious House of Worth et Bobergh opened in 1858. Its co-founder, Charles Frederick Worth, is largely thought of as the father of haute couture. He was one of a select few designers in the mid-19th century who offered original designs that anticipated the desires of their clientele. In this way, Worth transcended the trade of a dressmaker, who simply followed instructions given by a client, to become a fashion designer. A long-established institution today, the idea was a novel one in the 1860s, when Worth soared to international fame and celebrity on the merit of his design talent and his distinguished clientele, which included members of the aristocracy, such as Princess von Metternich and Empress Eugénie. After the retirement of his partner, Otto Bobergh, in the 1870s, both of Worth's sons joined the business, and the house continued to operate as 'Worth' under two subsequent generations of Worth men.

Above Maurice Taquoy, *Gazette du Bon Ton* (Gazette of Good Taste), 1912, issue 2; 'At Chamonix. Men's and Women's Suits for the Winter Sports'.

FAITES ENTRER !

Robe de dîner de Dœuillet

Opposite Javier Francisco Gosé, *Gazette du Bon Ton* (Gazette of Good Taste), 1912, issue 2; 'Have Them Come In! Dinner Dress by Dœuillet'.

Below, left Robert Dammy, *Gazette du Bon Ton* (Gazette of Good Taste), 1912, issue 2; 'Evening Falls. . .Evening Dress by Doucet'.

Below, right Pierre Brissaud, *Gazette du Bon Ton* (Gazette of Good Taste), 1912, issue 2; 'Between Dog and Wolves. City Dress by Worth'.

The witty character of *Gazette du Bon Ton* is perfectly captured in the title of this plate. An elegant woman crossing the Place Vendôme finds herself captured between her fashionable toy dog and the wolves roaming the urban landscape: well-dressed, handsome men.

LE SOIR TOMBE...
Robe du soir de Doucet

ENTRE CHIEN ET LOUPS
Robe de ville de Worth

LE JEU DES GRACES

Robe d'après-midi de Paquin

LA BELLE ET LA BÊTE
Matinée

Opposite George Barbier, *Gazette du Bon Ton* (Gazette of Good Taste), 1913, issue 7; 'The Graces' Game. Afternoon Dress by Paquin'.

Right, above Charles Martin, *Gazette du Bon Ton* (Gazette of Good Taste), 1913, issue 3; 'The Beauty and the Beast. Morning'.

Right, below Unsigned, *Gazette du Bon Ton* (Gazette of Good Taste), 1913, issue 6; 'A Farewell in the Night. Evening Dress by Paquin'.

L'ADIEU DANS LA NUIT
Robe du soir de Paquin

LES CERISES

Toilette de campagne par Paul Poiret

Georges Lepape, *Gazette du Bon Ton* (Gazette of Good Taste),
1913, issue 7; 'Cherries. Countryside Outfit by Paul Poiret'.

LE BEL ÉTÉ

Robe de lingerie pour la campagne

Louis Strimpl, *Gazette du Bon Ton* (Gazette of Good Taste),
1913, issue 9; 'The Beautiful Summer. Lingerie Dress
for the Countryside'.

SUR LA FALAISE

QUE C'EST BEAU LA MER!

Left, above Francisco Javier Gosé, *Gazette du Bon Ton* (Gazette of Good Taste), 1913, issue 10; 'On the Cliff. Summer Dress by Redfern'.

Left Pierre Brissaud, *Gazette du Bon Ton* (Gazette of Good Taste), 1913, issue 9; 'How Beautiful the Sea Is! Beach Dress by Chéruit'.

Opposite Pierre Brissaud, *Gazette du Bon Ton* (Gazette of Good Taste), 1913, issue 8; 'Let's Go! Let's Be Brave! Bathing Costume'.

This plate's caption, 'Du Courage!', underscores the model's daring choice of ensemble. In the 1910s such an expanse of bare leg would still have been perceived as an affront to female modesty. Swimsuits of the 19th and early 20th centuries were made from cumbersome wool and were worn with bloomers that extended to or past the knee, in addition to stockings.

Art, Fashions, Frivolities

L'OISEAU BLEU

Manteau du soir de Doucet

Jacques Drésa, *Gazette du Bon Ton* (Gazette
of Good Taste), 1913, issue 9; 'The Blue
Bird. Evening Coat by Doucet'.

LA SOURIS

Costume tailleur de Doucet

Jacques Drésa, *Gazette du Bon Ton* (Gazette of Good Taste), 1913, issue 11; 'The Mouse. Tailored Suit by Doucet'.

AH! LE BEL OISEAU!

Robe d'intérieur de Doucet

ON AURAIT PU NOUS INVITER AUSSI...

Robes d'après-midi et robe du soir de Doucet

QUI DOIS-JE ANNONCER ?

Robe de visites de Chéruit

L'ENTR'ACTE

Robe du soir de Worth

AU JARDIN DES HESPÉRIDES

Tailleur de Paquin pour l'automne

Previous pages, left Robert Dammy, *Gazette du Bon Ton* (Gazette of Good Taste), 1913, issue 12; 'Ah! The Beautiful Bird! Interior Dress by Doucet'.

Previous pages, right (top) Pierre Brissaud, *Gazette du Bon Ton* (Gazette of Good Taste), 1914, issue 6; 'They Could Have Invited Us Too. . .Afternoon Dresses and Evening Dress by Doucet'.

Previous pages, right (bottom left) Pierre Brissaud, *Gazette du Bon Ton* (Gazette of Good Taste), 1914,

issue 2; 'Whom Shall I Announce? Visiting Dress by Chéruit'.

Previous pages, right (bottom right) Maurice Taquoy, *Gazette du Bon Ton* (Gazette of Good Taste), 1913, issue 12; 'The Interval. Evening Dress by Worth'.

Above George Barbier, *Gazette du Bon Ton* (Gazette of Good Taste), 1913, issue 11; 'In the Garden of Hesperides. Autumn Tailored Suit by Paquin'.

Opposite Georges Lepape, *Gazette du Bon Ton* (Gazette

of Good Taste), 1913, issue 11; '"Which One?" Evening Dress by Paul Poiret'.

This silk-satin evening gown embodies two Poiret characteristics: a flair for the exotic East and the 'Iribe' rose. At least three versions of the dress with its 'lampshade' kimono-style bodice are known to exist today, in the Museum at the Fashion Institute of Technology, New York, the Chicago Historical Society and the Victoria and Albert Museum, London.

LAQUELLE ?
Robe de soirée de Paul Poiret

L'ENCENS, LE CIN

Ro

E ET LA MYRRHE

soir

S'IL NE VIENT PAS, NOUS SERONS TREIZE...

Robe de dîner de Doucet

LA DERNIÈRE ROSE

Robe d'après-midi de Redfern

IL A ÉTÉ PRIMÉ

Robe du soir

Previous pages Louis Strimpl, *Gazette du Bon Ton* (Gazette of Good Taste), 1914, issue 1; 'Incense, Cinnamon and Myrrh. Evening Dresses'.

The materialization of the 'Orientalist' aesthetic in fashion in the early 1910s was as alluring as it was controversial. It was often at odds with prevailing sartorial and gender norms, as well as with the nationalist pre-war attitudes. Still, revolutionaries in fashion design, such as Paul Poiret, embraced the exotic, and championed the turban and the harem trouser for their daring. Orientalism was subsequently welcomed by women of fashion, as well as by fashion illustrators – who adopted bold colour palettes and fantastical scenes for their own stylized interpretations, as exhibited here.

Above, left Jacques Drésa, *Gazette du Bon Ton* (Gazette of Good Taste), 1914, issue 2; 'If He Doesn't Come, There Will Be Thirteen of Us. Dinner Dress by Doucet'.

Above, right Francisco Javier Gosé, *Gazette du Bon Ton* (Gazette of Good Taste), 1913, issue 2; 'The Last Rose. Afternoon Dress by Redfern'.

Left Francisco Javier Gosé, *Gazette du Bon Ton* (Gazette of Good Taste), 1914, issue 3; 'He Won a Prize. Evening Dress'.

Opposite Louis Strimpl, *Gazette du Bon Ton* (Gazette of Good Taste), 1914, issue 2; 'The New Frisson. Tango Dress by Redfern'.

Tango madness swept Paris in 1913. The sultry, passionate dance, which originated in the slums of Buenos Aires, crossed the Atlantic with wealthy Argentines who came to Paris to patronize the couture houses. The physical intimacy between a man and woman required by the steps induced the ire of French cardinals, who denounced it as 'wanton and offensive' and forbade it to devout Catholics. Despite religious and moral objections, the tango flourished in the upper echelons of French society, spawning specialized tango dresses with more accommodating hems and no trains to allow fancy footwork.

"SALOMÉ"

Robe du soir de Paul Poiret

LA FLEUR MERVEILLEUSE

Robe du soir de Doucet

LE LYS ROUGE

Robe du soir de Paul Poiret

Above, left Robert Dammy, *Gazette du Bon Ton* (Gazette of Good Taste), 1914, issue 3; 'The Wonderful Flower. Evening Dress by Doucet'.

Above, right Simon Puget, *Gazette du Bon Ton* (Gazette of Good Taste), 1914, issue 4; 'The Red Lily. Evening Dress by Paul Poiret'.

Right Louis Strimpl, *Gazette du Bon Ton* (Gazette of Good Taste), 1914, issue 3; 'Black Smoke. Evening Dress by Redfern'.

Opposite Simon Puget, *Gazette du Bon Ton* (Gazette of Good Taste), 1914, issue 3; 'Salome. Evening Dress by Paul Poiret'.

LA FUMÉE NOIRE

Robe du soir de Redfern

Jean-Louis Boussingault, *Gazette du Bon Ton* (Gazette of Good Taste), 1914, issue 6; 'Dresses by Paul Poiret According to Boussingault'.

Guest artist Jean-Louis Boussingault's abstracted, geometric rendering has a strong Cubist influence, a first for the magazine and something of which it was very proud: 'The *Gazette du Bon Ton* remains in its role as witness to the elegant and artistic life of the time in publishing this plate,' it proclaimed to its readers. Cubism continued to inform the *Gazette*'s unique artistic ethos throughout the magazine's run.

Top George Barbier, *Gazette du Bon Ton* (Gazette of Good Taste), 1914, issue 6; 'Isola Bella. Evening Dresses by Redfern'.

Above George Barbier, *Gazette du Bon Ton* (Gazette of Good Taste), 1915, issues 8–9; 'Vichy II or the Puppet Game. From left to right: Callot, Jenny, Paquin, Martial et Armand, Callot, Dœuillet, Lanvin, Lanvin, Paquin and Lanvin'.

Opposite André Édouard Marty, *Gazette du Bon Ton* (Gazette of Good Taste), 1914, issue 7; 'My Heart Is Sighing. . . Park Dress'.

These three plates illustrate the rapid shift in silhouette that took place between 1913 and 1915. The narrow, restrictive hobble skirt reached the pinnacle of its popularity in 1913, when it began to appear with the overskirt of the 'lampshade tunic'. The tunic gradually lengthened until it reached the ground, as shown in the plate by Marty, opposite. This intermediate phase, when two distinctive silhouettes collided, was very brief; with the outbreak of World War I, the shift in silhouette that had begun before the conflict was hastened by women's need for economy and a greater range of movement in their daily activities. That ultimately resulted in the dismissal of the narrow underskirt in favour of a shorter, flared skirt. The dramatic difference in silhouette is illustrated clearly in the two plates above.

EN SUIVANT LES OPÉRATIONS

Above Drian, *Gazette du Bon Ton* (Gazette of Good Taste), 1915, issues 8–9; 'Following the Operations'.

Opposite Pierre Brissaud, *Gazette du Bon Ton* (Gazette of Good Taste), 1914, issue 4; 'Cursed Wind! Morning Coat by Chéruit'.

L'ÉVENTAIL D'OR

Éventail et Bracelets

Above Georges Lepape, *Gazette du Bon Ton* (Gazette of Good Taste), 1920, issue 2; 'The Golden Fan. Fan and Bracelets'.

Georges Lepape's illustration of a quintessential 'flapper' exudes a demure sexuality. The term 'flapper' was used in the 1920s to describe a subculture of young women who enthusiastically proclaimed their new autonomy by flouting the social mores of the previous generation. The flapper smoked, drank alcohol, spent her evenings in nightclubs, had her hair cut short and – shockingly – used cosmetics. Liberally applied dark lipstick accentuated the coveted 'cupid's bow' mouth,

and eyes were heavy with shadow and kohl. The flapper's personality was not based on subtlety: *Vogue* even advised its readers in an article on 15 May 1920 that 'there is not a woman living who could not increase her piquancy and charm by a little dash of artificiality, for there is a lure, a fascinating flavour about it.'

Opposite Pierre Brissaud, *Gazette du Bon Ton* (Gazette of Good Taste), 1920, issue 2; 'The Visit. Afternoon Dress and Children's Dresses by Jeanne Lanvin'.

Many of Brissaud's fashion plates featuring the designs of Jeanne Lanvin show mothers and daughters – a

relationship at the heart of Lanvin's life. She began her career in millinery, a job that allowed her to support herself and her daughter, Marie-Blanche. In 1923 Paul Iribe immortalized the bond between Lanvin and Marie-Blanche in a stylized illustration in which Lanvin looks lovingly down at her daughter, clasping her hands. The motif eventually became the house's logo, and it remains so today, testament both to Lanvin's love for her daughter and to the brand's continued appreciation of its rich heritage.

SI ON RENTRAIT GOUTER...
Tailleur et Robes d'enfant, de Jeanne Lanvin

RENTRONS
Robe de plage, de Beer

LE RETOUR DES AUTANS
Tailleur et Robe d'après-midi, de Dœuillet

Above, left Pierre Brissaud, *Gazette du Bon Ton* (Gazette of Good Taste), 1920, issue 9; 'What if We Went Home for Tea? Tailored Suit and Children's Dresses by Jeanne Lanvin'.

Above, right Pierre Brissaud, *Gazette du Bon Ton* (Gazette of Good Taste), 1920, issue 4; 'Let's Go Back. Beach Dress by Beer'.

Left Fernand Siméon, *Gazette du Bon Ton* (Gazette of Good Taste), 1920, issue 7; 'The Return of the Southerly Winds. Tailored Suit and Afternoon Dress, by Dœuillet'.

Opposite Eduardo García Benito, *Gazette du Bon Ton* (Gazette of Good Taste), 1920, issue 7; 'Tea Time. Fur Coat by Jeanne Lanvin'.

L'HEURE DU THÉ

Manteau de fourrure, de Jeanne Lanvin

EN PLEIN COEUR

ROBE DU SOIR, DE PAUL POIRET

Opposite Charles Martin, *Gazette du Bon Ton* (Gazette of Good
Taste), 1920, issue 10; 'The Woman who Died of Love.
Fashions and Manners by Torquate'.

Above André Édouard Marty, *Gazette du Bon Ton* (Gazette of Good
Taste), 1922, issue 2; 'Right Through the Heart. Evening Dress
by Paul Poiret'.

FUMÉE

ROBE DU SOIR, DE BEER

Art, Fashions, Frivolities

L'ÉPOUSÉE AUX DENTELLES
ROBE DE MARIÉE, DE WORTH

PENSE-T-IL A MOI ?
ROBE, DE PAUL POIRET

Above, left Alexander Rzewuski, *Gazette du Bon Ton* (Gazette of Good Taste), 1921, issue 2; 'The Bride and her Lace. Wedding Dress by Worth'.

Above, right André Édouard Marty, *Gazette du Bon Ton* (Gazette of Good Taste), 1921, issue 5; 'Does He Think of Me? Dress by Paul Poiret'.

Opposite George Barbier, *Gazette du Bon Ton* (Gazette of Good Taste), 1921, issue 1; 'Smoke. Evening Dress by Beer'.

LE BASSIN D'ARGENT

Robe de dîner garnie de ruban

LA DAME AU LÉVRIER

TAILLEUR, DE BEER

LES FLEURS DU VOISIN

Robe de Garden-Party

Above, left Eduardo García Benito, *Gazette du Bon Ton* (Gazette of Good Taste), 1920, issue 1; 'The Silver Basin. Dinner Dress with Ribbons'.

Above, right Eduardo García Benito, *Gazette du Bon Ton* (Gazette of Good Taste), 1921, issue 2; 'The Lady with the Greyhound'.

Greyhounds are a leitmotif in the illustrations of Eduardo García Benito, their sleek contours and elegant stature no doubt intended to complement the fashionable figure of their mistress. Another of Benito's greyhounds appears on page 227, in the plate entitled 'Diane', and there is another on the cover he designed for the catalogue for Paul Poiret's Spring 1917 ready-to-wear collection, which was created for the American market.

The tailored two-piece suit or *tailleur* in sombre shades of grey, blue and black became a necessary – and ubiquitous – part of women's fashion during the war, so much so that it remained a staple of women's dress after the end of the conflict. On 1 January 1919 *Vogue* observed that 'the little grey "tailleurs" are becoming so omnipresent in Paris that they suggest a uniform.' Women's continued use of the sleek but simple ensemble was testament to the changed attitudes in dress that espoused the benefits of uncomplicated, graceful garments. Such ideals would come to define the sportswear of designers such as Coco Chanel in the 1920s.

Left Robert Bonfils, *Gazette du Bon Ton* (Gazette of Good Taste), 1920, issue 3; 'The Neighbour's Flowers. Garden-Party Dress'.

Opposite Marcelle Pichon, *Gazette du Bon Ton* (Gazette of Good Taste), 1921, issue 6; 'The Arbour. Garden-Party Dresses'.

LA TONNELLE.

ROBES DE GARDEN-PARTY

LES NEIGES

Costume pour les sports d'hiver, en " agnella " de Rodier

LA LEÇON DE NATATION

COSTUME ET CHALE, POUR LE BAIN

LE COCU MAGNIFIQUE

ROBE EN TAFFETAS IMPRIMÉ, DE BIANCHINI

Above, left Maurice Leroy, *Gazette du Bon Ton* (Gazette of Good Taste), 1920, issue 9; 'The Snows. Winter-Sports Suit Made of "Agnella", by Rodier'.

Above, right Fernand Siméon, *Gazette du Bon Ton* (Gazette of Good Taste), 1921, issue 6; 'The Swimming Lesson. Bathing Suit and Shawl'.

Left Fernand Siméon, *Gazette du Bon Ton* (Gazette of Good Taste), 1922, issue 4; 'The Magnificent Cuckold. Printed-Taffeta Dress by Bianchini'.

The printed taffeta of this woman's dress bears all the hallmarks of a textile designed by Raoul Dufy. During the 1910s and 1920s, following his brief period of work with Paul Poiret, Dufy created spirited woodcut motifs for the manufacturer Bianchini; flowers, animals and scenes of daily life were signatures. In his autobiography *King of Fashion*, Poiret recalled how the two were working together at the small textile-printing facility they had only recently set up, when they saw 'the immense, looming silhouette of M. Bianchini. . .who came to propose to Dufy that he should provide him with more worthy industrial facilities. Dufy was gentleman enough not to accept without informing me of the proposition which had been made to him, and I a grandee not to prevent him from furthering his career.' The designs executed under the Dufy/Bianchini collaboration remain so definitive within the genre of Art Deco textile design that the firm still produces twenty of Dufy's motifs, in various colourways.

Opposite Robert Bonfils, *Gazette du Bon Ton* (Gazette of Good Taste), 1921, issue 10; 'The Horn Sounds. Hunting Dress'.

LES CINQ SENS
I. — L'ODORAT
CHAPEAUX, DE CAMILLE ROGER

LE LYS NOIR
ROBE DU SOIR, DE MADELEINE VIONNET

Nº 5 de la Gazette. Année 1923. Planche 24
Modèle déposé. Reproduction interdite.

"J'AI FAILLI ATTENDRE"
COSTUME VESTON, DE LUS ET BEFVE

Above, left Pierre Mourgue, *Gazette du Bon Ton* (Gazette of Good Taste), 1922, issue 7; 'The Five Senses – 1. Smell. Hats by Camille Roger'.

Camille Roger, who opened her doors in 1885, was one of the first modistes to hang her sign on the shopping thoroughfare of the rue de la Paix in Paris. Her kindness and generosity were nearly as famous as the quality of her hats, which were considered some of the finest in Paris. Following Roger's death in 1905, the house went through a series of female directors before its head milliner, Madame Prisca – who had been with the house for more than twenty years – was chosen to take the helm. In direct defiance of the 1920s vogue for the small, felt cloche, Prisca declared herself its 'avowed enemy', and asserted the influence of the house of Camille Roger to revive the fashion for fancifully trimmed hats, such as the two seen here.

Above, right Thayaht, *Gazette du Bon Ton* (Gazette of Good Taste), 1923, issue 5; 'The Black Lily. Evening Dress by Madeleine Vionnet'.

Left René Préjélan, *Gazette du Bon Ton* (Gazette of Good Taste), 1922, issue 4; 'I Almost Waited. Tailored Suit by Lus et Befve'.

Opposite Thayaht, *Gazette du Bon Ton* (Gazette of Good Taste), 1922, issue 5; 'A Memory of Easter in Rome. Afternoon Dress by Madeleine Vionnet'.

Thayaht, the moniker for the Italian artist and textile designer Ernesto Michahelles, was a close collaborator with Madeleine Vionnet between 1919 and 1924. During an extended trip to Paris, the twenty-six-year-old Thayaht sold designs to the houses of Worth and Vionnet, which had only recently reopened after World War I. Thayaht went on to design Vionnet's logo, and, working from Italy, was contracted to the house as a freelance designer and illustrator. His letter of engagement from 1922 read: 'I grant you the exclusive use of my designs for couture, and I will come to Paris twice a year for two months to work with Mme Madeleine Vionnet on the creation of her collection of models. . .I will also contribute to the *Gazette du Bon Ton* in your name. Aside from this, I shall retain my full artistic freedom.'

SOUVENIR DE PAQUES A ROME

ROBE D'APRÈS-MIDI, DE MADELEINE VIONNET

FAITES-MOI CELLE-CI

ROBE DU SOIR, DE DŒUILLET

de la Gazette du Bon Ton.   Année 1921.·— Planc¦

LE MIGNON PETIT SOULIER

MODÈLES DE PERUGIA

de la Gazette.   Année 1924-1925. — Planch¦

Above, left Pierre Brissaud, *Gazette du Bon Ton* (Gazette of Good Taste), 1921, issue 7; 'Make This One for Me. Evening Dress by Dœuillet'.

The elite social status enjoyed by fashion models today is a relatively new phenomenon. An article on the Parisian couture industry in *Everybody's Magazine* in October 1905 shed light on the profession of French models, who were called *mannequins*: 'In the main, mannequins are very ordinary young women whose history is but the history of the average Parisian working girl. . .a more ordinary-looking group of girls than the mannequins of a house when they arrive in the morning it would be hard to find, and a passer-by would not give them a second look; but when, a half hour later, Mademoiselle, perfectly corseted, skillfully made up as to complexion, eyes, and brows, with her hair dressed in the latest fashion, her nails and hands beautifully cared for, her feet clad in dainty high-heel slippers, sweeps across the showroom, wearing with true French grace a gown that is a thing of beauty – then the Paris mannequin is quite another proposition. She is not beautiful, but one forgets it; for she is excessively chic.'

Above, right Jean Grangier, *Gazette du Bon Ton* (Gazette of Good Taste), 1924–25, issue 2; 'The Lovely Little Shoe. Models by Perugia'.

Following his service in World War I, the French cobbler André Perugia reopened his business on the French Riviera. Hemlines had risen dramatically during the war and shoes, once obscured by long skirts, became an important element of a woman's ensemble. Perugia seized this opportunity to transform himself into one of the great designers of women's footwear, re-imagining women's shoes, once bland and formulaic, as tiny platforms of self-expression. Perugia experimented with previously unthinkable colour palettes, as well as new shapes and materials, including snake and lizard skin, which he is credited with introducing into the shoemaking trade. His flamboyant and unusual designs were embraced by the smart set holidaying in the south of France. Paul Poiret was so impressed by Perugia's innovation that he exhibited his shoes in the Poiret salons in 1921, cementing the shoe designer's place in the world of Parisian fashion. Perugia moved his operations to Paris in 1922, and by 1927 his designs had become so popular that he estimated that for every ten pairs of shoes he sold, 'eight are destined to be copied, legitimately or otherwise' ('Fashion: The House of Perugia', *Vogue*, 15 June 1927, 134).

Opposite George Barbier, *Gazette du Bon Ton* (Gazette of Good Taste), 1924–25, issue 4; 'Artemis. Coat by Worth'.

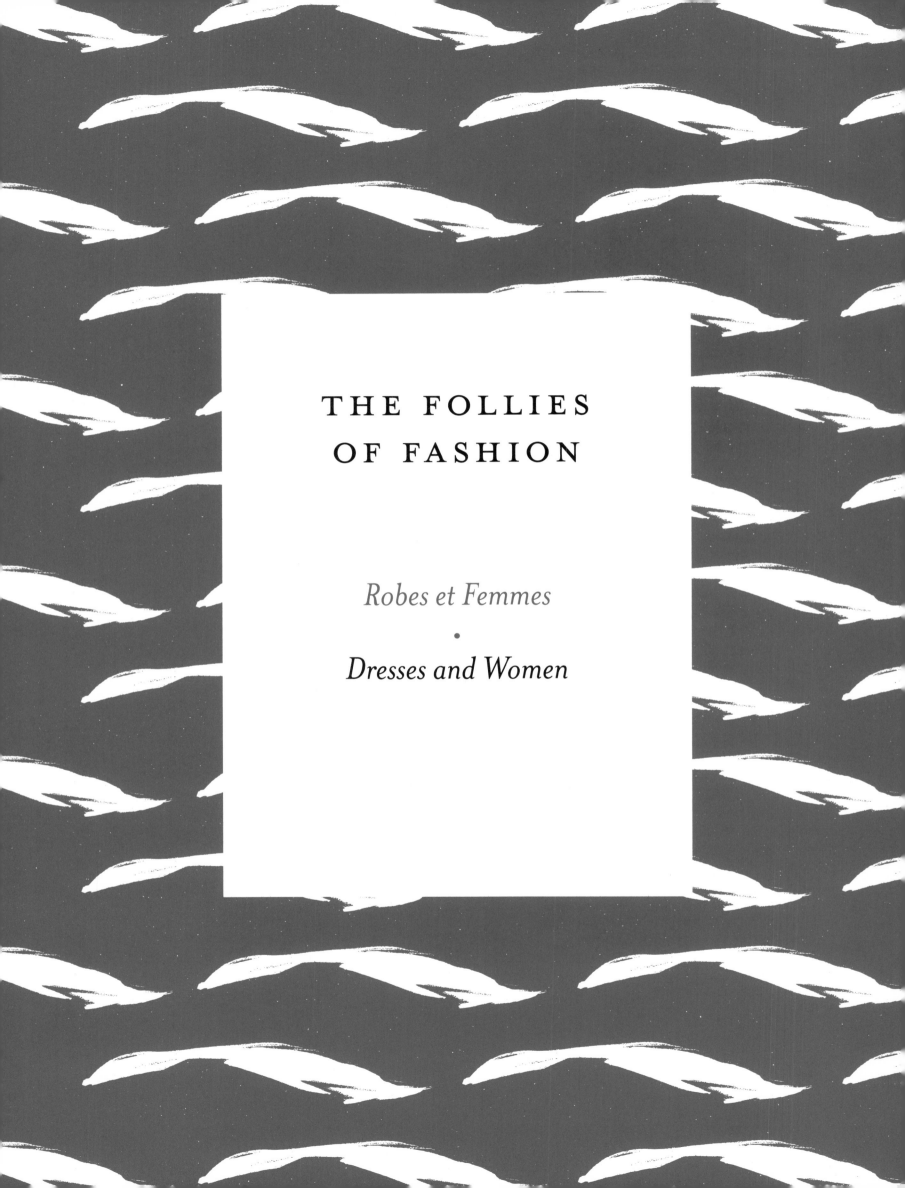

THE FOLLIES OF FASHION

Robes et Femmes

·

Dresses and Women

8

'Torture has not been abolished in France, it has only changed its name, today we call it Fashion.'
Cham [Charles Amédée de Noé], *c.* 1857[1]

The folly of the 'fashion victim' has been a rich source of material for satirists for hundreds of years. This genre of prints was well-established – and beloved – by the 18th century. In his treatise of 1788 on the art of caricature, the Englishman Francis Grose relishes the theme of the fashion faux pas, recommending to amateur artists that 'nothing affords greater scope for ludicrous representations than the universal rage with which particular fashions of dress are followed by persons of ranks, ages, sizes, and makes, without the least attention to their figures or stations.'[2] Enrico Sacchetti's album *Robes et Femmes* follows in this grand tradition of the comedic skewering of conspicuous consumption.

Produced in a limited edition of 300 in 1913, Sacchetti's work represented a marked departure from previous satirical fashion prints. Such prints often included pieces of coarse or witty text that elucidated the humorous nature of the scenes depicted. In choosing to omit these textual elements, Sacchetti followed in the footsteps of *Les Robes de Paul Poiret* (1908) in the positioning of the portfolio as an artist's publication. Before this, the public typically consumed fashion satire through newspapers, weeklies or individual prints sold in print shops. These individual prints were immensely popular, and some were issued as part of an ongoing series, as in the case of *Le Bon Genre*, whose plates form a collection of sardonic images depicting contemporary fashions, social customs and mores practised by a cast of archetypal characters.

One of the first practitioners of caricature was Leonardo da Vinci, who in the 15th century was producing studies of exaggerated facial features; over time the term 'caricature' came to be used for 'a variety of works depicting exaggerated faces, extreme physiques, fantastic forms composed of inanimate objects, and even animals acting like humans'.[3] Many of the same compositional devices are used in the creation of graphic satire, which is distinguished from caricature by an additional layer of meaning intended to convey moral judgment. Satire relies for its success on the viewer's knowledge of current events, politics and social trends. Elements of comedy and farce may be added to these references, formulaically, through the juxtaposition of various shapes and sizes, the introduction of anachronism and national stereotypes, or the irreverent treatment of venerated objects.[4] When done well, graphic satire holds the potential to be more pointed and cutting than thousands of words contained in a written manifesto.

By the time of *Robes et Femmes*, Sacchetti was already well versed in the art of social and political satire. Born in Italy in 1877, he spent his youth in the art-saturated environment of Florence, graduating with a degree in mathematics and physics from the city's Istituto Tecnico. As a designer he was largely self-taught, but during an apprenticeship with the artist Lorenzo Gelati in Milan, he designed covers for sheet music and contributed clever and caustic illustrations to such Italian journals as *Verde Azzurro* (1903–4) and *Teatro Illustrato* (1905–6).

In 1912, after a short stint working in Argentina as a caricaturist for the newspaper *El Diario*, Sacchetti moved to Paris, where he began his brief but brilliant career in

fashion. After a friend introduced him to the couturiers Gaston and Jean-Philippe Worth, his career followed a new direction for two years. His first commission in Paris was to 'design on swan skin a dozen fans' for the House of Worth.[5] Sacchetti said of his first encounter with the world of haute couture: 'I went to the great Maison de Couture on the rue de la Paix so I could see how things were made[;] there I glimpsed the tip of the strange abyss, so full of mystery, that is fashion.'[6] The fashion illustrations he went on to create for French magazines such as *La Vie Parisienne* are characterized by a sort of bemused detachment from the pursuit of high style, an idea he would realize more fully with *Robes et Femmes*.

In the early 1910s, the latest fashions were often the subject of international headlines and public raillery. The 'hobble' skirt, which the *New York Times* called 'the latest freak in woman's fashion', was a favourite target owing to its sheer impracticality.[7] With hems less than 1 metre (1 yard) in circumference, the new ultra-narrow silhouette seriously impeded a woman's movement; some women even wore elastic shackles called hobble garters just below their knees, to prevent themselves from ripping their dresses by taking too great a stride.[8] The irony that many of these women were active supporters of the Suffrage movement did not escape the notice of critics:

> If women want to run for Governor they ought to be able to run for a car [tram]. If they want to step into a President's chair they ought to be able to step into a motor. If they want to be legally free

> they shouldn't be sartorially shackled. But with the lack of logic that the sex can be counted on to display they have chosen a trammeled figure and shackled ankles when they need most to have them free in the strenuous race for equality with the trousered sex.[9]

Politics aside, women were widely cautioned by the fashion press against the slavish adoption of radical styles. Even Poiret, who was responsible for the hobble skirt and other 'extreme' fashions of the period lampooned in *Robes et Femmes*, advised women to be thoughtful in their selection:

> Do not sacrifice your beauty in a vain attempt at being fashionable. What does it matter if tight skirts be the fashion if your figure demands a wide one? Is it not important to dress so as to bring out your good points rather than to reveal the bad? Can any idea of being fashionable make up for the fact of being ridiculous?[10]

Although the eleven plates created by Sacchetti refer to (and critique) many of Poiret's fashion 'innovations', the two artists do share common ground in their call for the cultivation of good taste. Sacchetti's brand of satire here is sublimely subtle. One wonders if he points the accusing finger at the fashion designers and milliners for the outlandishness of their creations, or if the penchant for excess lies with the client who fails to show restraint in her enthusiasm for the trappings of luxury: velvet, fur, silks, brocades and breathtakingly expensive feathers. The garments consume the women, and Sacchetti has rendered them unrecognizable, their faces hidden or their backs turned. Their individuality has been sacrificed on the altar of fashion as they clownishly and mimetically select styles for novelty rather than suitability. Sacchetti's knowledge of the history of graphic satire is evident in his compositional choices; in plate 9 (see page 198) he juxtaposes a thin woman with a corpulent one, pointing out the appropriateness of certain styles for certain body types. He twists, morphs and distorts the fashionable silhouette to appear plant- or insect-like, a tactic the illustrator SEM would borrow the following year in his better-known satirical album *Le Vrai et le Faux Chic* (right).

Of all the artists and illustrators whose work appears in this book, Sacchetti's use of the pochoir technique is one of the most unusual. His illustration style is free-flowing and elastic. His colour palette, which at first seems to have been chosen with gleeful abandon, is on further inspection calculated – both his Italian heritage and the influence of Georges Lepape have been cited as contributing to Sacchetti's inspired use of colour in *Robes et Femmes*. The texture of the fabrics, furs and feathers is highlighted by the layering of transparent and opaque pigments by the colourists who translated his original works into pochoir prints, with the liberal addition of handwork. Among his renowned French counterparts, Sacchetti quickly gained a reputation for his facility as a fashion illustrator, and before he returned to Italy at the outbreak of war in 1914, art critics had recognized that 'the most original and the strongest of all those Parisians was an Italian.'[11]

Top SEM, *Le Vrai et le Faux Chic* (True and False Chic), 1914; page 34.

Above SEM, *Le Vrai et le Faux Chic* (True and False Chic), 1914; page 4.

Opposite, left Enrico Sacchetti, *Robes et Femmes* (Dresses and Women), 1913; cover.

Opposite, right Enrico Sacchetti, *Robes et Femmes* (Dresses and Women), 1913; imprint page.

1.   Cham [Charles Amédée de Noé], *Les Tortures de la Mode* (Paris, [1857?]), 1.
2.   Francis Grose, *Rules for Drawing Caricaturas: With an Essay on Comic Painting* (London, 1788), 4
3.   Constance C. McPhee and Nadine M. Orenstein, *Infinite Jest: Caricature and Satire from Leonardo to Levine* (New York, 2011), 3.
4.   *Rules for Drawing Caricaturas*, 28–33.
5.   Caterina Zappia, *Mostra di Enrico Sacchetti: Ritratti, Moda, Illustrazioni* (Legnano, Italy, 1989), 9.
6.   Quoted in *ibid.*, 20.
7.   '"The Hobble" is the Latest Freak in Woman's Fashions', *New York Times*, 12 June 1910, SM10.
8.   'The Hobble Garter', *Pittsburgh Press*, 7 October 1910.
9.   '"The Hobble" is the Latest Freak in Woman's Fashions'.
10. Florence Hull Winterburn, Jean-Philippe Worth and Paul Poiret, *Principles of Correct Dress* (New York and London, 1914), 240–41
11. *Mostra di Enrico Sacchetti*, 21.

Enrico Sacchetti, *Robes et Femmes* (Dresses and Women), 1913;
plate 6 (in two parts).

While the edition of *Robes et Femmes* was limited to 300 copies,
announcements of its release were placed in fashion magazines
and other luxury titles, including *Gazette du Bon Ton*, where it was
advertised for the price of thirty francs.

Enrico Sacchetti, *Robes et Femmes* (Dresses and Women), 1913;
plates 11 (above left), 4 (above right) and 3 (opposite).

The satire in the illustration opposite is the most pointed in
all of Sacchetti's illustrations for *Robes et Femmes*. The ostentation
of the cumbersome ensemble modelled by the woman in the
foreground stands in stark contrast to the simplicity of the
other's jaunty, menswear-inspired suit, which would become
a staple of women's wardrobes after World War I.

Enrico Sacchetti, *Robes et Femmes* (Dresses
and Women), 1913; plate 7.

The Follies of Fashion

Enrico Sacchetti, *Robes et Femmes* (Dresses
and Women), 1913; plate 8.

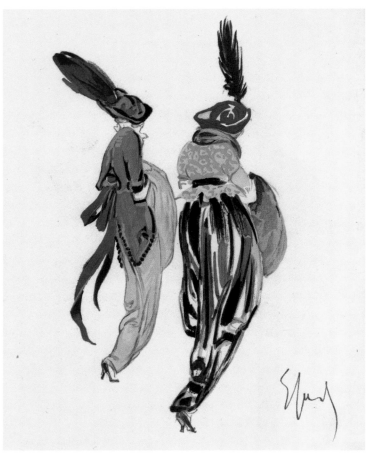

Enrico Sacchetti, *Robes et Femmes* (Dresses and Women), 1913;
plates 10 (top left), 9 (top right), 2 (above left), 5 (above right)
and 1 (opposite).

The Follies of Fashion

AT WAR
WITH FASHION

Le Goût du Jour

•

In Style

9

'In war, everything is remade...' [1]

The inaugural issue of *Le Goût du Jour* was printed in November 1918, the same month as the sound of French cannon rang through Paris's streets in joyous celebration of the Allied Forces' victory in World War I.[2] It had been more than four years since war had broken out in July 1914 and prompted an unceremonious end to the Belle Époque (the forty-year period of peace and prosperity that produced a terrific flowering of the arts and sciences). The careless frivolities and indulgences that had been enjoyed for decades were replaced abruptly by struggle and sacrifice in the most gruesome war Europe had yet known. Those in the fashion and luxury industries were faced almost immediately with a struggle for survival; such overt displays of extravagance were at direct odds with the harsh reality of wartime life. Despite this, Parisian couture was able to continue production almost entirely unscathed, upheld not only by the dedication of its largely female workforce but also by the industry's intimate correlation with French patriotism. Its success became a marker of France's continued role as a world leader in culture and taste despite the war. The continued operation of the luxury book industry was justified along the same lines, but to the virtual exclusion of fashion publications.[3]

Journal des Dames et des Modes (see chapter 6), the little periodical that originally dated back to 1797, ceased publication in the summer of 1914, never to return, while *Gazette du Bon Ton* (see chapter 7) suspended production for six years, returning in 1920. The publisher of the latter, Lucien Vogel, served in the French military in Morocco, a fate shared by many of the regular artist/illustrator contributors to his magazine, who were also at their nation's service.[4]

The artist André Édouard Marty, while recovering from wounds received at the front, filled his time sketching life in the hospital ward. His recuperation is evidenced by his contribution to the 1919 issue of *Modes et Manières d'Aujourd'hui* (which was actually published in 1921). As a largely sedentary process, stencilling was a viable profession for men who had returned from the war with injuries that precluded them from certain types of employment. A poignant intersection of ex-soldiers and the printing technique became a reality in 1918 on the rue Friant, when the Patria printing studio set up a program specifically to train and employ disabled war veterans in the art of pochoir.[5]

The printer and publisher François Bernouard began *Le Goût du Jour* in 1918 with the hopeful enthusiasm that his publication would fill a void left by the luxury fashion periodicals that had disappeared during the war. His magazine was intended as a 'renovation of one of the noblest traditions in France', an homage to the little fashion journals of yore.[6] The first issue was produced in an edition of 510 and proudly proclaimed its artistic intentions by announcing that no paid advertising would appear in its pages. This sacrifice of income for the sake of artistic integrity is perhaps the reason that the second issue was not published until June 1920. This time, Bernouard created a larger, fortnightly print run with three tiers of editions, which ranged in price from 250 to 800 francs for an annual subscription of twenty-four issues.[7] An article on inflation in France's postwar economy in the *New York Times* in 1920 perhaps best puts the exorbitance of these sums in context, citing the average cost of a man's ready-to-wear suit as 450 francs and of a custom, made-to-measure suit as 700 francs.[8]

Le Goût du Jour

à Paris, en Décembre 1918

Dessin de Monsieur DRÉSA

Robe de petit dîner

Toque de peluche noir garnie de singe — Robe de satin bleu-nuit à panneaux coulissés en voile de soie bleu de chine, bordée de franges de singe — Ceinture de satin bleu-nuit.

Dessin de Monsieur Georges BONFILS

Pyjama

Chemise de soie blanche flottante, sans boutons — Pantalon en soie de chine, blanc ou bleu-marine — Ceinture en pareille.

Above Robert Bonfils, *Le Goût du Jour* (In Style), December 1918, page 5; 'Pyjama. Floating white-silk shirt, without buttons – China-silk trousers, white or navy blue – matching belt'.

Despite the somewhat feminine features of the figure's face, this image portrays a soldier who has recently returned from war. He has shed his tall black boots and uniform of French blue and red (pictured at the plate's lower left), and returned to the comforts of home in a set of silk lounging pyjamas.

Left Jacques Drésa, *Le Goût du Jour* (In Style), December 1918, cover; 'Small-Dinner Dress. Soft hat trimmed with monkey fur – dark-blue satin dress, with China-blue silk net panels, trimmed with monkey fur – dark-blue satin belt'.

At War with Fashion

That Bernouard drew inspiration for *Le Goût du Jour* from its well-known predecessor *Journal des Dames et des Modes* is undeniable. Both publications featured just eight pages of text on the theatre, art, poetry and fashion, contributed by well-known artists and writers of the day, and a selection of between two and four fashion plates per issue. Bernouard turned to many of the artists who had formerly been in the employ of *Journal des Dames et des Modes* and *Gazette du Bon Ton* before the war. A comparison of Maurice Taquoy's work for *Journal* (see page 117) and *Le Goût du Jour* (see page 207) reveals that Bernouard copied the formula of the *Journal des Dames et des Modes* plates down to the precise dimensions, double-lined border and placement of text.

By keeping to a familiar structure, the *Goût du Jour* plates managed to retain some of the romance associated with fashion plates of an already bygone era, but it cannot be said that they are supreme expressions of the pochoir medium. The illustrations in *Le Goût* are markedly restrained and use colour very minimally, a reflection of the shift that occurred in fashion illustration during the war, now informed by abstract art movements, notably Cubism. This evolution in illustrative style did not necessarily lend itself to the diverse capabilities of the refined pochoir technique. This, paired with the quick and often careless application of the pochoir process in many instances, renders the plates of *Le Goût du Jour* visually wanting, especially when compared to its rival pochoir publication *Gazette du bon ton*. Marcelle Pichon's 'suggestion for a dress' on page 209 has been given only the most basic washes of pigment: a pale pink for the sheer voile dress, a spritely chartreuse for the hat and an unmemorable, limp grey for the cape. The overall effect is underwhelming given Pichon's exceptionally strong understanding of colour, as demonstrated by her work in other publications from the same period. Her plate 'The Arbour', which appeared in *Gazette du bon ton* the following year (page 181), recalls the scintillating colour palettes of the Fauves with its juxtaposition of hot pinks, electric blues and deep, dark olive greens.

Likewise, Pierre Brissaud's plate featuring a woman in a rose-coloured taffeta evening dress (page 216) is notable for its lack of background. One of Brissaud's gifts as an illustrator was his ability to convey a story through the complex, immersive environments he created in his fashion plates. Brissaud's plate of 1921 for *Gazette du Bon Ton*, depicting the interior of a Parisian couture house (page 187), swiftly and deftly pulls the viewer in to the haute-couture shopping experience. This type of advanced composition was not apparently of interest to the publisher Bernouard, nor did his coloristes implement any of the advanced pochoir techniques that could be used to create gradients, textures or the illusion of depth.

Paris was on its feet once again by 1920, and the ensuing decade would be one of unbridled decadence. Ultimately, Bernouard's little journal would not survive past the year's end. *Gazette du Bon Ton* had returned to the market in 1920 with a quality of pochoir plates that was infinitely superior to those of *Le Goût du Jour*. This, coupled with *Le Goût*'s exorbitant cost – which was well above or on par with its competitor – was surely a factor in the demise of the magazine. Bernouard would only ever publish fourteen issues of *Le Goût du Jour*, and just three complete runs are known to exist in museum or library collections worldwide, making this title prized for its exquisite rarity.

1. Claude Lepape and Thierry Defert, trans. Jane Brenton, *From the Ballets Russes to Vogue: The Art of Georges Lepape* (New York, 1984), 80.

2. *Le Goût du Jour*, December 1918, 18.

3. Georges Lecomte, 'A New Period of Fine Printing in France', *Art and Life* XI/6 (December 1919), 320. The article discusses the 'patriotic courage and faith' of the planners of various exhibitions of 'traditional and modern' books during the war. No luxury fashion publications appear to have been printed during the war, with the exception of a special issue of *Gazette du Bon Ton* highlighting the Panama Pacific International Exposition in San Francisco, held in 1915 to support Parisian haute couture.

4. *From the Ballets Russes to Vogue*, 82–86. Vogel's attempts to enlist in the French armed forces were at first rejected because he was born in Alsace, which had become part of Germany at the end of the Franco-Prussian war in 1871; Alsace would once again become part of France in 1918, at the end of World War I.

5. *Le Goût du Jour*, December 1918, 16. See also V. Fauchier-Magnan, 'Nouveaux Papiers Coloriés Français', *La Renaissance de l'Art Français et des Industries de Luxe*, I, March 1918, 17–19.

6. *Le Goût du Jour*, 20 June 1920, 1.

7. The complete edition of 1,432 issues was broken down into three tiers: seven editions on China paper for the price of 800 francs; twenty-five editions with the plates on China paper and the remainder of the issue on Arches paper for 400 francs; and 1,400 editions entirely on Arches paper.

8. Edwin L. James, 'French Poor Feel Pinch of New Taxes', *New York Times*, 3 January 1920.

Robe de jardin en taffetas blanc, jupe froncée, broderies de paille bleue, châle de dentelle.

Cape de soie plissée montée sur empiècement brodé et plissé.

Above, left Hélène Perdriat, *Le Goût du Jour* (In Style), July 1920; 'White-Taffeta Garden Dress, Gathered Skirt, Blue Straw Embroidery, Lace Shawl'.

The artist Hélène Perdriat first began illustrating at the age of twenty-one while suffering from a life-threatening illness. After her recovery, she continued to work as an illustrator and became well-known for her evocative and emotionally complex portraits of women, no doubt reflecting her own personal experiences. In her day she was one of the most recognized female artists working in France, and her name was frequently mentioned in the press alongside that of her fellow French painter Marie Laurencin, who also favoured the feminine face as subject matter. Perdriat's work may be distinguished from Laurencin's, however, by its 'keen and vivacious sense of humour' ('Art Notes', *New York Times*, 7 December 1916).

Above, right Llano Flores, *Le Goût du Jour* (In Style), July 1920; 'Pleated Silk Cape on an Embroidered and Pleated Yoke'.

Opposite Eduardo García Benito, *Le Goût du Jour* (In Style), June 1920; 'Blue-Silk Pyjama with Silver Facing, Black Silhouettes. Lamée Silver Hussar Culotte'.

Pyjama en soie bleue, revers d'argent, silhouettes noires.
Culotte hussarde lamée d'argent.

*Cuirasse en écailles clair de lune, jupe en soufflé
de soie rose ibis, chûte de fleurs.*

Robe de chambre de soie fulgurante, jaune serin Parements et col de seduisia quadrillée dans le ton.

Complet veston ton clair, pardessus d'été tête de nègre

Robe de satin, jupe brodée d'une fine soutache remontant en bretelle sur le corsage.

Above, left Eduardo García Benito, *Le Goût du Jour* (In Style), July 1920; 'Canary-Yellow, "Fulgurante"-Silk Dressing Gown. Matching Square-Patterned Seduisia Facing and Collar'.

Above, right Maurice Taquoy, *Le Goût du Jour* (In Style), August 1920; 'Light-Coloured Three-Piece Suit, Dark-Brown Summer Overcoat'.

Left Llano Flores, *Le Goût du Jour* (In Style), August 1920; 'Satin Dress, Skirt Embroidered with a Slim Braid Reaching up to the Bodice as a Strap'.

Opposite Janine Aghion, *Le Goût du Jour* (In Style), August 1920; 'Moonlight-Shells Breastplate, Ibis-Pink "Soufflé"-Silk Skirt, Cascade of Flowers'.

Robe de jeune fille, organdi jaune soufre, cape en mousseline à reflet vert jade, rubans de velours noir.

Suggestion pour une robe, voilée et retroussée sous un gros nœud de ruban.

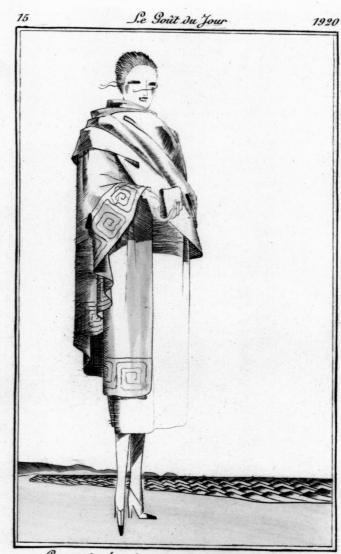

Cape de kashangora rejetée sur l'épaule, garnitures de ruban ciré.

Opposite Robert Bonfils, *Le Goût du Jour* (In Style), August 1920; 'Young Girl's Dress, Sulphur-yellow Organdie, Green Muslin Cape with Jade-green Gleams, Black-velvet Ribbons'.

Many of the fashion plates by Robert Bonfils show the influence of Cubism and Futurism in their portrayal of speed and movement. This plate is particularly unusual as in it, Bonfils quite literally breaks a centuries-old fashion-plate tradition that confined an illustration within a clearly demarcated border. The butterfly featured here goes outside the plate's borders,

a harbinger of the freer style of fashion illustration that developed in the 1940s and 1950s.

Above, left Marcelle Pichon, *Le Goût du Jour* (In Style), August 1920; 'Suggestion for a Dress Veiled and Rolled up under a Large Ribbon Bow'.

Above, right Llano Flores, *Le Goût du Jour* (In Style), September 1920; 'Kashangora Cape Thrown over the Shoulder, Waxed-ribbon Ornaments'.

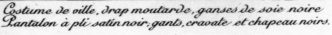

Costume de ville, drap moutarde, ganses de soie noire Pantalon à pli satin noir; gants, cravate et chapeau noirs.

Cape et robe plissées et brodées en serge ivoire

Above, left Charles Guérin, *Le Goût du Jour* (In Style), September 1920; 'City Suit, Mustard-coloured Wool, Black-silk Braid. Black-satin Pleated Trousers, Black Gloves, Tie and Hat.

A city look for women featuring trousers, as seen here, would have been considered truly radical in 1920. Trousers had been adopted by women for country and sporting use – and the kinship of this ensemble with the riding habit is undeniable – but to wear them in town verged on scandalous. It would be two years before such 'progressive organizations' as the American Designers' Association would advocate for everyday use of knickerbockers, and much longer still for full-length trousers.

Above, right Hélène Perdriat, *Le Goût du Jour* (In Style), September 1920; 'Cape and Dress, Pleated and Embroidered in Ivory Twill'.

Opposite Georges Gorvel, *Le Goût du Jour* (In Style), September 1920; 'Canary-yellow "Frisson" Taffeta Tea Dress, with Monkey-fur Trim'.

London's Great Exhibition of 1851 introduced monkey fur to Western markets. Its long, black shag made it a novelty in the fur trade, and new materials of any kind were quickly embraced within the fashion world. By the 1890s monkey fur was in great demand for muffs and trims. Both the canary-yellow tea gown seen here and the white suit designed by Jeanne Lanvin depicted on page 174 are trimmed with monkey fur.

Overleaf (left) Llano Flores, *Le Goût du Jour* (In Style), October 1920; 'Antelope Gloves with Moleskin Appliqué, and Antelope Gloves with Coloured Facing and Lines'.

Overleaf (right) Llano Flores, *Le Goût du Jour* (In Style), November 1920; 'Fan-bags, One Enhanced with Exotic Birds' Feathers, with a Diamond Arrow Pinned In'.

Robe pour le thé, en taffetas frisson jaune serin, garnie de singe.

Gants d'antilope avec applications de taupe et gants d'antilope avec revers et baguettes de couleur.

Sacs éventail, l'un rehaussé de plumes d'oiseaux
des Îles, avec, épinglée une flèche de diamants.

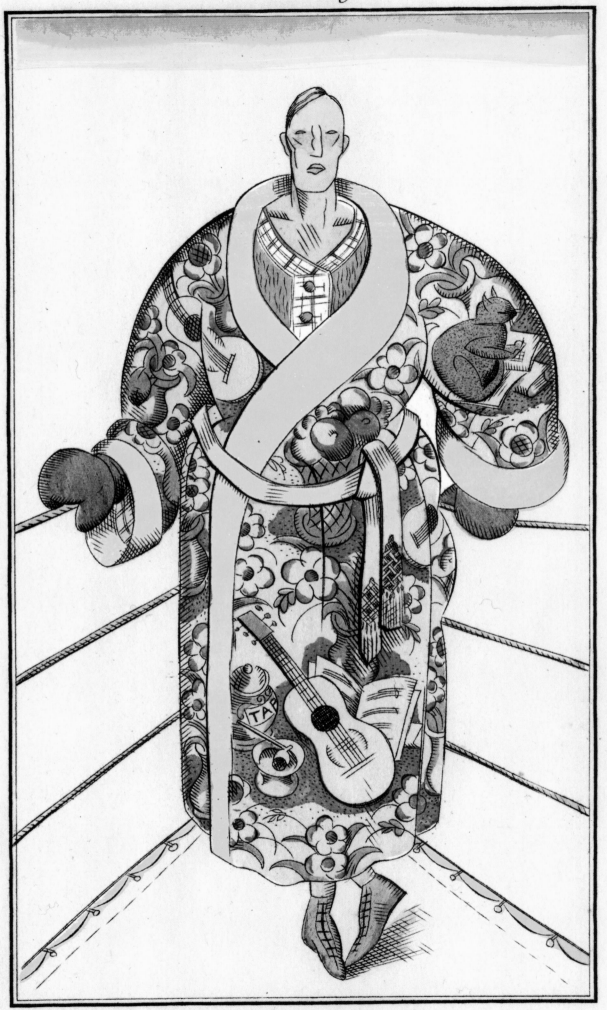

Peignoir de boxe en brocart: "les plaisirs de l'intimité"
Revers de soie jaune

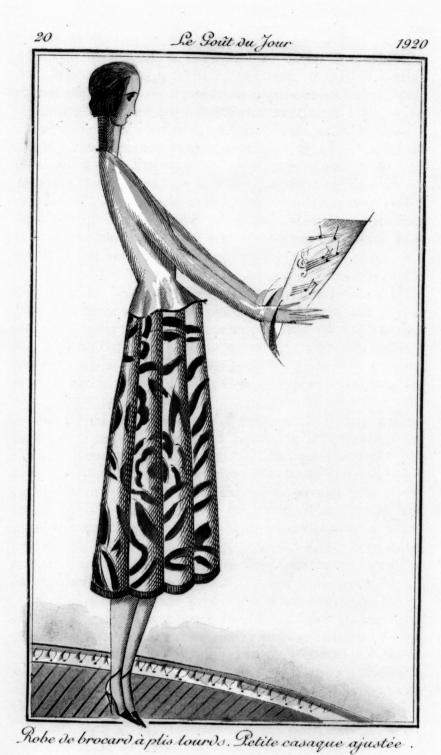

Robe de brocard à plis lourds. Petite casaque ajustée.

Pardessus court en mousse avec col Kamchatka

Manteau de chasse en kaska couleur d'automne avec col et parements en daim.

Above Marcelle Pichon, *Le Goût du Jour* (In Style), September 1920; 'Brocade Dress with Heavy Pleats. Small Close-fitting Blouse'.

Top right Marcelle Pichon, *Le Goût du Jour* (In Style), October 1920; 'Short Foam Overcoat with Kamchatka Collar'.

Right Llano Flores, *Le Goût du Jour* (In Style), October 1920; 'Autumn-Coloured Kaska Hunting Coat with Suede Collar and Facing'.

Opposite Jean-Gabriel Daragnès, *Le Goût du Jour* (In Style), November 1920; 'Brocade Boxing Dressing Gown: "The Pleasures of Intimacy". Yellow Silk Facing'.

Robe du soir en taffetas rose
Ceinture en ruban

Tailleur breton garni d'un col en renard,
parements de mousseline blanche. Gilet brodé,
guêtres de drap jaune.

Above, left Pierre Brissaud, *Le Goût du Jour* (In Style), December 1920; 'Pink Taffeta Evening Dress. Ribbon Belt'.

Above, right Robert Bonfils, *Le Goût du Jour* (In Style), October 1920; 'Breton Tailored Suit with a Fox Collar, White Muslin Facing. Embroidered Waistcoat, Yellow Wool Gaiters'.

Opposite Mme Léon Cheriane, *Le Goût du Jour* (In Style), December 1920; 'Evening Dress'. The basketweave on the bodice of this dress does little to conceal the woman's breasts.

Such a racy design was not intended for fashionable dress, but would have been worn as a stage costume by a performer in one of Paris's many topless revues. The fact that this woman is an actress or dancer is further indicated by the fact that she is positioned between a set of curtains, holding a bouquet of flowers given to her, no doubt, by a gentleman admirer.

Robe pour le soir.

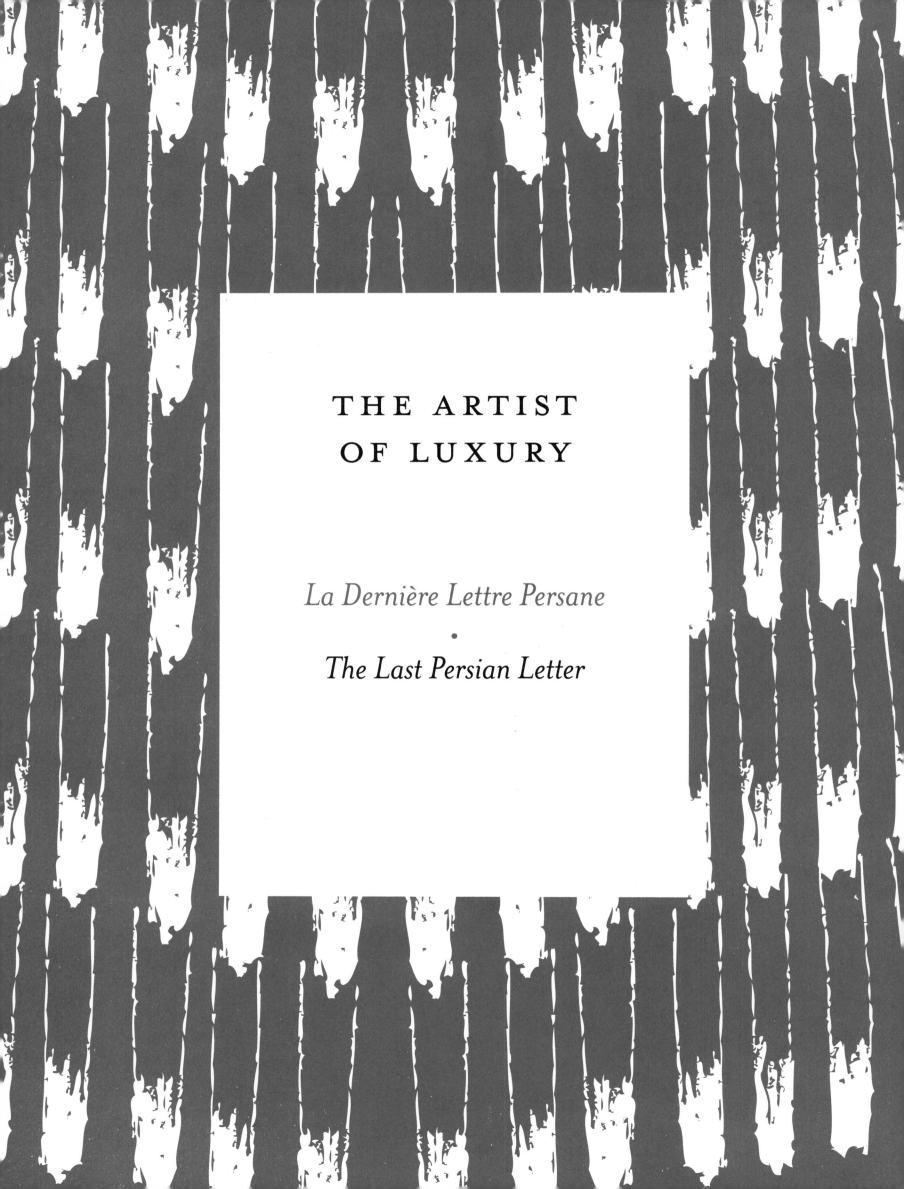

THE ARTIST OF LUXURY

La Dernière Lettre Persane

·

The Last Persian Letter

10

'Art is nothing more than the human desire to prolong, to fix for eternity, fleeting moments of extraordinary beauty. To me, the beauty of women and flowers are the greatest, most exquisite wonders of the world.'
Eduardo García Benito[1]

The talents of two Spanish artists were brought together in 1920 to create the opulent gold-leaf and pochoir album *La Dernière Lettre Persane*. Commissioned by the elite French furrier Fourrures Max, Eduardo García Benito's stylized illustrations of women in fine furs are prefaced by an original text by the novelist Miguel Zamacoïs. The work's title, which translates as 'The Last Persian Letter', is a reference to a novel of 1721 by the French philosopher Montesquieu, *Les Lettres Persanes*, which served as its inspiration. The book is ostensibly structured as a series of letters exchanged with the friends and family of the characters Usbek and Rica, two Persian noblemen visiting France in the early 18th century. Through the eyes of these fictional foreigners, Montesquieu offers a social critique of his own time, touching on such diverse topics as the state of the French economy, Christianity and international affairs. Nearly 200 years later, Zamacoïs conceived *La Dernière Lettre Persane* similarly, as a letter written by Usbek to his beloved Zobéide, who had remained behind in his Persian seraglio while he travelled to France.

The album opens with the explication:

I know my little Zobéide, nervous and impatient as one of those strange Siamese cats listening to the singing in the foliage without noticing the coveted bird. . . .And it is to soften the punishment of her wait that I asked an artist well-known here, the painter Benito, to interpret for the eyes of a spoiled child, in Persian style, some of the adornments that I find both typical and original.[2]

A five-page letter follows, nestled within black and gold borders that depict scenes of the hunt and the hunted. The letter describes to Zobéide the innate finesse Parisian women had for arraying themselves in the 'lustrous and silky skins. . .of sable, ermine [and] chinchilla'.[3] Usbek tells her: 'Fur is not, for French women, like it is for us at home, a simple preservative against the cold or a vague and parsimonious trim, it comprises the most ravishing and the most sumptuous ornamentation. It is very frequent to see here elegant and rich women prefer furs over jewels.'[4] And indeed, the most coveted and rare specimens of animal furs at this time commanded staggering sums on a par with the finest gemstones.

At the beginning of the 20th century, the most expensive French furriers included the legendary Revillon and – by comparison – a relative fledgling to the trade, Fourrures Max.[5] The latter was singularly run by Madame André Leroy, who took over the company after the death of her business partner in World War I. Of all the French fur designers, Leroy was 'the one associated most closely with the modernistic', so her selection of Benito as illustrator of *La Dernière Lettre Persane* falls in line with the house's reputation for producing *le dernier cri*.[6] Known professionally as simply 'Benito', the young Spaniard arrived in Paris in 1912 at the age of twenty-one after his home town of Valladolid granted its prodigiously talented native son a full scholarship to study art at L'École des Beaux-Arts. Immediately after arriving there, Benito fell into a circle of avant-garde

FOURRURES MAX
19, Avenue Matignon

Les nouveaux
Salons d'essayage

Draeger, Imp.

With and at Paul Poiret's, I began painting women. Since I had been painting matadors before, the 'chicness' came easily for me. Everyone in Spain knows the difference between a village's matador and a professional one. And well, that is the difference between an elegant woman and one that is not, or is less so. Thanks to Paul Poiret, I learned to appreciate that subtlety. This, I think, is what brought me the contracts with the American magazines.[10]

These magazines included *Femina*, *Gazette du Bon Ton*, *Vogue* and *Vanity Fair*; for the last two publications combined, he created more than 100 covers over the course of his career.

The working relationship between Benito and Poiret dates back at least to the years of World War I, when Benito provided illustrations for a catalogue of Poiret's Spring 1917 ready-to-wear collection, which was sold exclusively in America.[11] The two friends may have joined forces once again on *La Dernière Lettre Persane*, as Poiret's biographer Palmer White attributes the design of the furs featured in the Fourrures Max album to Poiret.[12] Curiously, Poiret's name does not appear in the folio's credits, but an established industry practice existed whereby leading furriers partnered with couturiers who functioned as consultants on the collections that bore the fur houses' labels.[13]

Benito's woodblock prints featuring 'ravishing and dangerous felines' – as Zamacoïs described the fur-clad women – are luxuriously augmented with gold-leaf and pochoir colouration. In each of the album's twelve plates, a single female figure is centred on an otherwise blank page; only two plates give the merest hint of a background: curtains frame the sloping golden shoulders of the woman in the plate entitled 'Noailles Duc', while a canine companion gazes adoringly up at 'Diane'. The titles bestowed on each illustration underscore the inherent exoticism of the album's premise, and while some, such as 'Scheherazade' and 'Geisha', are explicit in their references to the Far East, the majority allude to European history and myth; the vogue for Orientalism had faded quickly with the outbreak of World War I. After the war, illustration techniques shifted from the fantastic towards more concrete, linear forms: 'Young artists were turning away from the decorative curves and moving towards an altogether firmer style of drawing. Angles and volumes recovered their rightful place. Even colours changed. Where once were blues, emeralds and carmines, now it was all black and white, brown and cream.' Despite the new favour for the angular – straight lines, V-shapes, rectangles and octagons – the dominant feeling remained 'one of grace, and amid the shadows of Cubism there appears a young woman, graceful as flesh itself and tender as a rose.'[14]

Benito's fluency in Cubism is evident in his flat, two-dimensional renderings of the women in furs, the silhouettes distilled to only the most essential shapes. Their hard-edged geometry is a natural match for the unbroken planes of colour fundamental to the pochoir process, which

Spanish artists working in France, including Pablo Picasso and Juan Gris. The important exhibition of Cubist painters, the 'Salon de la Section d'Or', took place within a few months of his arrival, and the young art student found himself profoundly influenced by the radical fracturing of form in Marcel Duchamp's *Nude Descending a Staircase*. Not long after completing his studies, Benito began to gain professional recognition as a painter working in the Cubist and Fauvist manners;[7] his first exhibition took place in Paris in 1917, and the following year his work was shown at the Salon d'Automne.[8]

These triumphs in the realm of academic painting were mere markers on Benito's professional trajectory, however. He credited his first commercial success to a series of World War I-themed prints published from 1914 to 1918 and created in the tradition of *images d'Epinal*. 'This edition was such a success that it made a name for me in Paris,' he recalled. 'I soon had a reputation of a man of good taste, and the very next night [after its release] I began to receive invitations to exhibition openings, theatre premiers, literary salons and offers from other publishers.'[9] This early success secured Benito's entry into the world of high society – and high fashion, a part played in no small measure by his close personal friend and collaborator Paul Poiret. Not only did Poiret introduce the artist and illustrator to the American publishing magnate Condé Nast, at one of the elaborate soirées thrown at the Poiret couture house, but also he was Benito's usher into the intersecting worlds of art and fashion. Benito recalled:

has been implemented throughout the album with exceeding restraint; two plates do not feature pochoir at all, being entirely coloured in gold leaf, while the remaining plates incorporate pochoir colour in varying degrees. The women's stark contours and impossible proportions also owe a debt to the fashion-illustration innovations of Georges Lepape in *Les Choses de Paul Poiret* (1911; see chapter 2), as well as the work of Benito's fellow artist and cherished friend Amedeo Modigliani, who had only recently died, at the age of thirty-five, from tuberculosis and prolonged substance abuse. Modigliani's stylistic influence can be seen in the way in which Benito has elongated the women's bodies, optimizing the space available for the depiction of the fur garments. Their tiny heads have been sparsely rendered in a tender, yet stoic manner that recalls the abstract simplification of African masks, which were an ongoing source of inspiration for many Cubist artists.

The sense of exotic 'otherness' in *La Dernière Lettre Persane* is compounded by the rare and mysterious nature of the furs depicted in its pages. The exact type of pelt used is illegible in many of the plates, yet a handful clearly depict skins from faraway lands: ermine, chinchilla and leopard. For Zamacoïs, a fur coat unequivocally gave the feminine sex the 'allure of little beasts', and with the transformative act of slipping on her fur, a woman suddenly 'appears much like a cat, a panther, a little tigress, who in the phases of human evolution, suddenly remembers, simply with the touch of fur, a past life'.[15] The primal pleasure of wearing fur was hardly novel, for fur was then – and remains today – the world's first status symbol and luxury good. Amid the economic prosperity and exuberant excesses of the 1920s, the lavishness of fur creations reached unprecedented levels of decadence, and the art of their display was perfected by 'French women and Parisians in particular', who, in the estimation of the album's creators, added 'the grace to grace, the elegance to elegance and the chic to chic'.[16]

Opposite Fourrures Max advertisement, c. 1922.

Above Eduardo García Benito, *La Dernière Lettre Persane* (The Last Persian Letter), 1922; cover.

1. Quoted in María Teresa Ortega Coca et al., *Eduardo García Benito: Los años de Nueva York (1921–1940)* (Valladolid, Spain, 2009), 72.
2. Miguel Zamacoïs, *La Dernière Lettre Persane* (Paris, [1920?]), 2
3. *Ibid.*, 6. Zobéide is also the name of one of the lead characters in the Ballets Russes' production of *Schéhérazade*. The favourite of Shah Sharyar, Zobéide is one of several unfaithful wives who – in their husband's absence – bribe the head eunuch to allow their slave lovers into the harem for an orgy.
4. *Ibid.*, 5.
5. A review of French fashion periodicals finds the firm Fourrures Max first mentioned in 1904; Revillon was founded in 1723.
6. 'Fashion: Fourrures Max', *Vogue*, 15 March 1926. Translating as 'the latest cry', the French phrase *le dernier cri* is used to refer to the newest fashions and trends.
7. *Eduardo García Benito*, 51.
8. *Ibid.*, 48.
9. *Ibid.*, 75.
10. *Ibid.*
11. During World War I, Poiret was conscripted and worked as a military tailor, but continued to manoeuvre ways to keep his businesses alive. In 1917 he launched Poiret Inc. in the United States, to supply or license his perfumes and designs for clothing, furniture and decorative arts to select American boutiques and department stores. Poiret's American line consisted of fourteen 'original but simple' ready-to-wear looks at prices within the reach of the upper-middle-class American market, who were assured of the legitimacy of their purchase by the 'reproduction autorisée' Poiret label sewn into each garment. See Paul Poiret, *Les Modèles de Paul Poiret: Printemps 1917* (New York, 1917), 5.
12. Palmer White, *Poiret* (New York, 1973), 173–74, 176. This attribution is called into question by the fact that White does not cite a source for this information.
13. Edward Tarler, *The Truth About Furs* (New York, 1934), 7. The leading American furrier I. J. Fox worked with the couture houses Lanvin, Molyneux and Maggy Rouff in the development of their lines.
14. Henry Bidou, preface to Georges Lepape, *Costumes de Théâtre, Ballets & Divertissements* (Paris, 1920), 7.
15. *La Dernière Lettre Persane*, 7.
16. *Ibid.*, 6.

Eduardo García Benito, *La Dernière Lettre Persane* (The Last Persian Letter), 1922; 'Geisha' (above left), 'Idole' ('Idol'; above right) and 'Princesse lointaine' ('Faraway Princess'; opposite).

Each of the black spots seen on the coat opposite signifies a single ermine pelt. The fur of the ermine, also called the stoat, changes colour according to season as a form of camouflage: it is brown in the summer and white in the winter, and only the tip of its tail remains black year round.

The finest ermine skins at this time were imported from Russia, where the animal was trapped in the dead of winter in order to obtain striking black-and-white pelts. Because of the sheer number of pelts needed to create a garment, and the difficulties inherent in obtaining them, ermine was considered the ultimate luxury fur and was a favourite of royalty for centuries.

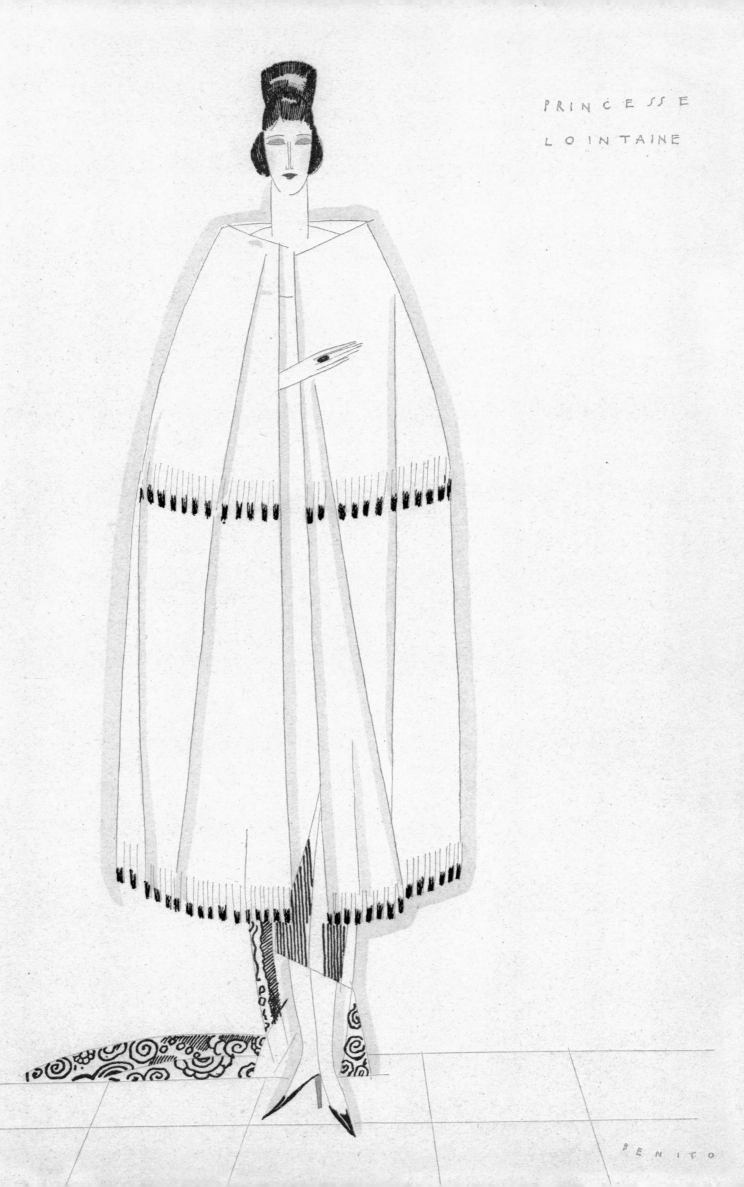

BENITO

TRIOMPHE

BENITO

La Dernière Lettre Persane

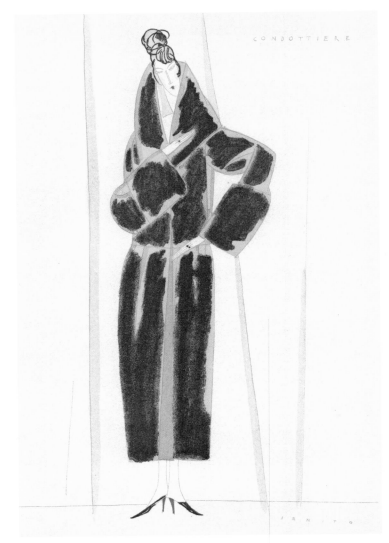

Eduardo García Benito, *La Dernière Lettre Persane* (The Last Persian Letter), 1922; 'Triomphe' ('Triumph'; previous pages, left), 'Noailles-Duc' (Duke of Noailles; previous pages, right), 'Goyesca' (above left), 'Condottière' (above right) and 'Diane' (opposite).

Above, left Shoes with red soles or heels have been a mark of prestige since the 17th century, when King Louis XIV passed an edict that granted members of his inner circle the right to wear red heels. Since that time, many shoe designers have followed in the royal footsteps, most famously Christian Louboutin, who denies that the signature red soles of his shoes have anything to do with history. He says the idea came to him when a lacklustre prototype of one of his designs arrived and, while pondering how to boost its appeal, he noticed a woman in the office painting her nails. After slathering the sole of the prototype in her red nail polish, Louboutin inaugurated the look as his brand identity.

Overleaf Eduardo García Benito, *La Dernière Lettre Persane* (The Last Persian Letter), 1922; 'Florentin' (left) and 'Scheherazade' (right).

Page 230 Eduardo García Benito, *La Dernière Lettre Persane* (The Last Persian Letter), 1922; 'Boabdil'.

The title 'Boabdil' refers to the 15th-century sultan Muhammad XI, the last Muslim ruler of Spain. Over the course of centuries, the plight of 'Boabdil', who was caught between the manipulations of a politically ambitious mother and the Muslim-Christian conflict, has been immortalized in a variety of literary and musical works, including a three-part opera.

Page 231 Eduardo García Benito, *La Dernière Lettre Persane* (The Last Persian Letter), 1922; 'Dogaresse'.

DIANE

FLORENTIN

The Artist of Luxury

La Dernière Lettre Persane

BOABDIL

BENITO

The Artist of Luxury

DOGARESSE

BENITO

BIOGRAPHICAL NOTES

FASHION HOUSES & COUTURIERS

Beer (c. 1891–1931)

The fashion house Beer was one of the four oldest in Paris, its only predecessors being Worth, Doucet and Paquin. The design philosophy of its founder, Gustave Beer, was 'conservative elegance for conservative customers', including the who's who of international royalty. The former czarina of Russia and the queens of Belgium, Italy and Romania were patrons of the house, which was reputed to charge the highest prices in Paris. It was known particularly for its evening gowns, furs and lingerie, and for the richness of its embroidery. Beer died in 1908, after which the house continued under the direction of Paul Trimbach and Monsieur Pierre, its head designer until the 1920s.

Bianchini-Férier (1889–)

The textile firm of Bianchini-Férier was founded in the city of Lyon, the centre of French luxury textile production since the days of Louis XIV. The company's innovative and novel fabrics set the industry standard, and it cultivated a close relationship with the couture industry. Many of its pioneering fabrics, such as silk charmeuse and crêpe georgette, were designed specifically for use in couture gowns. From 1912 to 1928 the company collaborated with the artist and designer Raoul Dufy, whose bold, distinctive patterns often played out on the pages of *Gazette du Bon Ton* (see page 183). The company survives to this day, albeit under a different name: it was taken over in 1992 by Tissages Baumann and later by Cédric Brochier.

Chéruit (c. 1906–35)

Chéruit, one of the premier couture houses of the early 20th century, was founded by Louise Chéruit in about 1906. It was an original sponsor of the *Gazette du Bon Ton*, and one of a handful of houses that remained open during World War I. In 1914 a scandal over her Austrian lover forced Chéruit to flee Paris, leaving her business in the hands of Julie Wormser and Louise Boulanger. The house remained open, under the direction of various designers, until 1935, when Elsa Schiaparelli took over the premises for her own couture business.

Marcelle Demay (1910–19)

As soon as she opened her Parisian atelier, the modiste Marcelle Demay garnered an international reputation as a premier millinery tastemaker. Her success was secured by an exclusive contract with the American department-store giant Wanamaker and high-profile relationships with celebrity clients. Demay documented her acute understanding of the power of celebrity in advertising in not one but two publications, *Nos Étoiles* (1911) and the pochoir-printed album *La Mode en mil neuf cent douze chez Marcelle Demay* (1912; see chapter 4). Little is known about Demay outside the small window of success she enjoyed during the 1910s. Her business survived the war, but appears to have closed soon afterwards.

Dœuillet (1900–c. 1930)

The couture house Dœuillet opened its doors in 1900 on the place Vendôme, Paris, the same year several of the house's debut designs were featured in the Exposition Universelle. The founder of the house, twenty-five-year-old Georges Dœuillet, had parlayed his former career as a silk merchant into his own business with the financial backing of Benjamin Guggenheim, which may explain why so many of Dœuillet's clients were wealthy American women. The house was especially known for its *robe de style*, the equivalent of the present-day cocktail dress.

Doucet (1871–c. 1930)

The firm known as Doucet was founded in about 1818 as a purveyor of lace and lingerie, and existed as a family enterprise until 1871, when Jacques Doucet converted it into a couture house. Many of Doucet's creations incorporated the fine lace for which the family business had been known, as well as beadwork and feathers. Some of the era's most famous women, including the actress Gabrielle Réjane and the celebrated courtesan Liane de Pougy, were patrons.

As an individual, Jacques Doucet cultivated the persona of a connoisseur: an oenophile, gourmand and important collector of 18th-century and modern art. That made a strong impression on the young Paul Poiret, who entered Doucet's employ in 1897, as would another future luminary of 20th-century fashion, Madeleine Vionnet, in 1907. By the 1920s, however, the house's relevance was declining, and in 1928, after Jacques's death, Doucet merged with Dœuillet to become Dœuillet-Doucet.

Fourrures Max (c. 1904–?)

Advertisements for the elite French furrier Fourrures Max began to appear in fashion magazines in about 1904, with an additional attribution to Leroy & Schmid. It is thought that M. Schmid was Mme André Leroy's business partner, who is known to have perished in World War I; after that, Mme Leroy served as the sole director and head designer of Fourrures Max. The house garnered a reputation for the ultra-modern aesthetic of its fur garments and the cutting-edge interiors of its Parisian fur salons. Original Fourrures Max creations, as well as adaptations of the house's designs, were sold in the United States at such high-end department stores as Saks Fifth Avenue and Bonwit Teller.

Lanvin (1890–)

The House of Lanvin began modestly. After training as a milliner in Paris and as a dressmaker in Barcelona, Jeanne Lanvin opened a millinery shop from her apartment on rue Boissy d'Anglas in 1890. When her marriage failed in 1903, Lanvin provided for herself and her young daughter, Marie-Blanche. Clients admired the clothes she made for her daughter, and her reputation as a dressmaker quickly spread. In 1909 Lanvin established itself formally as a couture house with departments for both women's and children's clothing, and it became known for its inspired use of colour and the youthfulness of its designs. In the 1920s the business expanded to include sportswear, menswear and an interior-design division. It maintained its official designation as a purveyor of haute couture until 1993, and today offers luxury ready-to-wear clothing, perfume and accessories.

Lucile, Lady Duff-Gordon (1863–1935)

Professionally known as Lucile, Lady Duff-Gordon was one of the early 20th century's great innovators in the business of fashion. Maison Lucile opened in 1894 in London. The designer was known for her outspoken, larger-than-life personality almost as much as for her designs for romantic chiffon dresses, diaphanous tea gowns and saucy lingerie. She was one of the first designers to capitalize on celebrity culture, and designed for the It girls of the day and the women of the Ziegfeld Follies. A consummate provocateur, Lucile gave her creations such innuendo-laden names as 'Her Climax' and 'The Garden of Love'.

With the financial backing of Lucile's second husband, Sir Cosmo Duff-Gordon, Maison Lucile went global; as Lucile Ltd it expanded to New York in 1909, and to Paris and Chicago in 1911. In 1916 she pioneered the diffusion line, collaborating with Sears, Roebuck & Co. to create mail-order versions of her designs, thus becoming the first couturière to launch a ready-to-wear line.

Paquin (1891–1956)

At its pinnacle, Paquin is estimated to have been the world's largest couture house, employing approximately 2,700 workers worldwide, with branches in Buenos Aires, London, Madrid and Paris, as well as fur salons in the United States. The firm was founded on the rue de la Paix in Paris by the husband-and-wife team Isidore and Jeanne Paquin, both experienced in the couture industry. Cutting-edge but never experimental, Paquin developed a reputation for its warm, hospitable client relations and unerringly chic garments. Jeanne led the house after Isidore's death in 1911, and was president of the couture industry's governing body during World War I. Following Jeanne's retirement in 1920, Madeleine Wallis served as the

house's head designer into the 1930s, and was succeeded by Ana de Pombo and Antonio Castillo, among others. In 1954 the house of Paquin merged with the world's oldest couture house, Worth, only to close its doors two years later.

André Perugia (1893–1977)

The shoemaker André Perugia is widely regarded as having introduced the element of fantasy into women's footwear. Trained by his father in the art of shoemaking from the age of eleven, Perugia took over his father's shop in Nice in 1913. He was called up a few months later, and his time in the military was spent working as an engineer in an aeroplane factory, during which he thought a great deal about the nature of design. When he reopened his shop after World War I, he at first produced the black, tan and beige shoes that were typical of the time. It was not until he rethought his designs, incorporating bright colours and such unusual materials as lizard and snakeskin, that his shoes captured the admiration of the elegant women holidaying on the French Riviera, and, later, of Paul Poiret, who introduced the Perugia brand to the world of Paris fashion in 1921.

Paul Poiret (1879–1944)

The French avant-garde couturier and fashion pioneer Paul Poiret was instrumental in the modernization of fashion design and illustration in the early 20th century. His pioneering pochoir-printed albums *Les Robes de Paul Poiret racontées par Paul Iribe* (1909; see chapter 1) and *Les Choses de Paul Poiret vues par Georges Lepape* (1911; see chapter 2) highlight his controversial but nevertheless revolutionary design aesthetic, a unique blend of Orientalist and Neoclassical influences that championed a natural expression of the body through uncorseted, columnar silhouettes. The two albums were instrumental in validating fashion illustration as a vehicle for artistic expression, and ushered in a new era of luxury fashion albums that would last until the 1920s when, perhaps ironically, the designer's influence waned. Poiret's design aesthetic did not translate into post-war modernist ideals, which emphasized simplicity and utility in dress, and his popularity diminished greatly, leading to the closure of his business in 1929.

Redfern (1881–1940)

The English couture house Redfern was founded in 1881 by John Redfern, and eventually opened branches in London, Edinburgh, New York and Paris. Redfern was a staple of the Parisian fashion scene, and was known especially for its tailor-made suits and other sportswear. The house was one of the founding sponsors of *Gazette du Bon Ton*.

Camille Roger (1885–1940s)

Camille Roger's eponymous millinery firm was for decades considered to be one of the finest hat-making establishments in Paris. Roger herself eschewed the limelight brought by the renown of her hats, and fostered a familial atmosphere within her establishment. She demanded of her employees – who were fiercely loyal – the highest quality of workmanship, and personally inspected each model produced. After her death in 1905, the house was led by a succession of female directors, most notably Madame Prisca during the 1920s and 1930s.

Madeleine Vionnet (1912–)
Widely considered by authorities on fashion to be one of the greatest fashion designers of the 20th century, Madeleine Vionnet was apprenticed at an early age to a dressmaker and later worked in Paquin's London salon and the Parisian couture houses Callot Sœurs and Doucet. In 1912 Vionnet opened her own couture house, but the venture was short-lived owing to the outbreak of World War I. Relaunched ten years later, the House of Vionnet introduced the bias-cut technique and stunned the fashion world with brilliant, geometrically complex designs that, once inhabited by a body, appeared fluid, easy and effortless.

Worth (1858–)
Generally agreed to be the father of haute couture, Charles Frederick Worth began his career in fashion working as a salesman for Gagelin-Opigez, a purveyor of high-end textiles, trimmings and mantles. In 1858, after being denied a promotion, Worth left the company and, with Otto Bobergh, established the couture house known until 1870 as Worth et Bobergh, and later as just Worth. The company's designation as an official supplier to Empress Eugénie of France in the 1860s cemented its status as a luminary of the Parisian fashion scene, and it became known especially for its formal court gowns. Following Charles's death in 1895, the house was directed by two subsequent generations of Worth men. By 1954 both its branches (in Paris and London) had merged with Paquin, which folded in 1956. The House of Worth continued to operate in subsequent decades under various owners, and in 2011 released its first ready-to-wear collection.

ILLUSTRATORS

Léon Bakst (1866–1924)
The Russian painter and costumier Léon Bakst is best known for his spectacular sets and costumes for the Ballets Russes, the famous Russian dance troupe that took Paris by storm in the early 20th century. Bakst's vast knowledge of history and world culture combined with his brilliant understanding of the decorative effect of colour to create visually delightful theatrical masterpieces that captured the artistic zeitgeist.

George Barbier (1882–1932)
One of the great French illustrators of the early 20th century, George Barbier was also a designer of costumes for theatre and ballet, a journalist and a writer. Born in Nantes, France, he studied at the École des Beaux-Arts in Paris, alongside many of the artists and illustrators later dubbed the 'Knights of the Bracelet' by *Vogue*, including Paul Iribe, Georges Lepape and Charles Martin. Over the course of his career, he contributed to many popular journals, including *Gazette du Bon Ton, Les Feuillets d'Art, Fémina, Vogue* and *Comœdia Illustré*. He created set designs and costumes for the Folies-Bergère, and worked as an illustrator for artists' books and *éditions de luxe*. Very little documentation of Barbier's personal life survives; he died at the age of fifty, at the pinnacle of his success.

Eduardo García Benito (1891–1981)
After being granted a scholarship by his home town of Valladolid, Spain, to study at the École des Beaux-Arts in Paris, Eduardo García Benito moved to that city in 1912. While studying there, he became part of a circle of Spanish artists that included Picasso and Juan Gris and was inspired by the nascent Cubist and Futurist art movements. A painter his whole life, Benito is best known for his illustration work for French and American publications – *Femina, Gazette du Bon Ton, Vogue* and *Vanity Fair* – which obliged him to divide his time between Paris and New York during the 1920s and 1930s. While he was in America, Hollywood celebrities, including the actress Gloria Swanson, employed him as an interior designer and portraitist. He returned to his roots for the last two decades of his life, and lived quietly as a painter in Valladolid.

Robert Bonfils (1886–1972)
In common with many of the artists that were his contemporaries, Robert Bonfils was a man of many talents. He enjoyed a notable career in the decorative arts, designing a range of products from fabrics to porcelains. As a fashion illustrator, he contributed to *Gazette du Bon Ton* and *Le Goût du Jour*, as well as *Modes et Manières d'Aujourd'hui*. But it is Bonfils's prolific body of work in luxury-edition books before and after World War II, as an engraver, binding designer and illustrator, that makes him one of the leading contributors to the Art Moderne and, later, Art Deco styles.

Bernard Boutet de Monvel (1884–1949)
The respected painter, engraver and illustrator Bernard Boutet de Monvel was one of the core contributors to *Gazette du Bon Ton* referred to as the 'Knights of the Bracelet'. His statuesque, often emotionless beauties are also to be found in other fashion publications, including *Journal des Dames et des Modes, Vogue* and *Harper's Bazaar*. After World War I he also worked as a society portraitist and interior designer in Europe and the United States.

Pierre Brissaud (1885–1964)
One of the more prolific illustrators of the early 20th century, Pierre Brissaud was part of the circle of bright

young illustrators dubbed the 'Knights of the Bracelet' by *Vogue*, a clique that included George Barbier, Paul Iribe, Georges Lepape, Charles Martin and Brissaud's first cousin Bernard Boutet de Monvel. Brissaud studied alongside these friends at the École des Beaux-Arts in Paris, and in the studio of Fernand Cormon. As well as contributing fashion illustrations to *Gazette du Bon Ton*, *Le Goût du Jour* and *Vogue*, he illustrated numerous books and worked in commercial advertising, creating illustrations for ad campaigns for Cadillac, Crisco and Steinway pianos, among others.

Umberto Brunelleschi (1879–1949)
The Italian artist Umberto Brunelleschi studied in Florence before moving at the turn of the 20th century to Paris, where he established himself as an artist of many talents. He worked as a fashionable portrait painter and graphic artist before expanding into fashion and book illustration, at which he enjoyed great success. He also worked as a designer of theatre sets and costumes, and his numerous credits in that field include designing costumes for Josephine Baker.

Jacques Drésa (1869–1929)
Born in Versailles, Jacques Drésa is best known for his textile and tapestry designs. One of the older and more frequent contributors to *Gazette du Bon Ton*, Drésa also designed sets and costumes for the Paris Opéra and the Théâtre des Arts.

Étienne Drian (1885–1961)
The artist Étienne Drian was a stalwart of fashion illustration during the 1910s and 1920s, and enjoyed international fame and success, notably through high-profile collaborations with such celebrities as Gaby Deslys and Cecile Sorel, whom he also called friends. Known simply as 'Drian', the moniker with which he signed his work, he illustrated for magazines including *Journal des Dames et des Modes*, *Gazette du Bon Ton*, *Vogue* and *Femina*. He also illustrated books, and designed sets and costumes for the Casino de Paris.

Marie-Madeleine Franc-Nohain (1878–1942)
The French illustrator Marie-Madeleine Franc-Nohain, née Dauphin, adopted the pen name of her husband (the lawyer and author Maurice-Étienne Legrand), Franc-Nohain, after their marriage in 1899. As well as contributing illustrations to *Journal des Dames et des Modes* and *Le Rire*, the mother of three became a well-known illustrator of children's books.

Francisco Javier Gosé (1876–1915)
The Spanish artist Francisco Javier Gosé, who received his artistic training in Barcelona, first visited Paris in 1900 to view the Exposition Universelle. Enraptured with Montparnasse's bohemian art scene, he lived alternately in Paris and Barcelona for the next fifteen years, working as a painter and illustrator. A regular contributor to the early issues of *Gazette du Bon Ton*, he is noticeably absent from the later editions; he suffered from a chronic respiratory condition and died in his home town of Lérida at the age of only thirty-nine.

Paul Iribe (1883–1935)
The Basque-French satirist and illustrator Paul Iribe also worked as an interior decorator and designer of furniture, textiles and jewelry. Born in Angoulême, France, he was educated in Paris, where he lived for most of his life. At first working in the realm of political and social satire, Iribe contributed his first illustration to *Le Rire* at the age of seventeen, and worked for *L'Assiette au beurre* before founding his own weekly satirical paper, *Le Témoin*, in 1906. His revolutionary designs for *Les Robes de Paul Poiret racontées par Paul Iribe* (1908; see chapter 1) marked a turning point in the history of fashion illustration. During the late 1910s and early 1920s, Iribe spent significant periods of time in America, designing costumes and sets for Hollywood productions. Returning to Paris in the 1930s, he worked on publishing projects, and designed a collection of fine jewelry for his then lover Gabrielle 'Coco' Chanel, who called him 'the most complicated man I ever knew'.

Georges Lepape (1887–1971)
The Parisian illustrator Georges Lepape was known for his collaboration with Paul Poiret on the album *Les Choses de Paul Poiret vues par Georges Lepape* (see chapter 2) and for his illustrated covers for the American, French and British editions of *Vogue*. He was born in Paris, where he lived throughout his life. He received his artistic training at the École des Beaux-Arts and studied in the atelier of the historical painter Fernand Cormon, where he formed friendships with leading artists of his generation. In 1911 Paul Poiret introduced Lepape to the world of fashion illustration and gave him complete artistic freedom in creating the album *Les Choses de Paul Poiret vues par Georges Lepape*. Lepape also contributed to *Gazette du Bon Ton*, *Modes et Manières d'Aujourd'hui*, *Harper's Bazaar* and *Femina*. After World War I, he taught for twelve years at the New York School of Fine and Applied Art in Paris.

Charles Martin (1884–1934)
Charles Martin was one of the core artistic contributors to *Gazette du Bon Ton*, who were known as the 'Knights of the Bracelet'. As a fashion illustrator, he contributed to such publications as Marcelle Demay's *La Mode en mil neuf cent douze chez Marcelle Demay* (1912; see chapter 4), *Modes et Manières d'Aujourd'hui* (1913) and *Journal des Dames et des Modes*, but he also established himself as a leading graphic artist and poster designer, as well as a designer of sets and costumes for ballet and the theatre. Perhaps more than that of any other illustrator of the period, Martin's style is distinctively Cubist. His most renowned work is the folio 'Sports et Divertissements' ('Sports and leisure'), in which his illustrations accompany short musical pieces by the composer Erik Satie on that theme.

André Édouard Marty (1882–1974)

The artist André Édouard Marty was one of the so-called 'Knights of the Bracelet', the core group of illustrators – and friends – at the heart of the magazine *Gazette du Bon Ton*. He was a premier, in-demand fashion illustrator whose romantic, often contemplative illustrations can also be found in *Modes et Manières d'Aujourd'hui*, *Femina*, *Vogue* and *Vanity Fair*, among many others. He served on the jury of the now famous Exposition Internationale des Arts Décoratifs et Industriels Modernes of 1925. He also gained prestige as an illustrator of books and posters during this period, and later as a set and costume designer for the theatre.

Hélène Perdriat (1894–1969)

It is thought that the artistic talent of Hélène Perdriat was discovered by the couturier and art collector Jacques Doucet. As a young woman, Perdriat had come to Paris from her home town of La Rochelle, in the hope of becoming a writer. After contracting consumption, and not expecting to survive, Perdriat felt compelled to create a self-portrait, which launched her artistic career. She was known especially for her paintings of women, but also worked as an illustrator, engraver and set and costume designer, as well as writing poetry.

Enrico Sacchetti (1877–1967)

Born in Rome, Enrico Sacchetti obeyed his father's wishes and obtained a degree in mathematics and physics, despite dreaming of becoming an artist. He gained informal art training by apprenticing himself to painters and printmakers in Florence, where he had studied. After working briefly as a satirical illustrator in Milan and in Argentina, Sacchetti found his way to Paris, where he was introduced to the world of fashion illustration in 1912, contributing to such periodicals as *Gazette du Bon Ton* and *La Vie Parisienne*. His album *Robes et Femmes* (see chapter 8), which satirized contemporary fashions of the day, was released in 1913. The outbreak of World War I forced Sacchetti back to Italy, where he continued to work as an illustrator of humorous journals, satirical newspapers and children's books.

Fernand Siméon (1884–1928)

A native of Paris, Siméon studied at the École des Arts Décoratifs there, and quickly became known for his facility in creating woodblock prints. The fashion illustrations he contributed to *Gazette du Bon Ton* and *Modes et Manières d'Aujourd'hui* were rendered as woodcuts and then printed using a combination of woodblock and pochoir processes. He created woodcut illustrations for dozens of books, including those by Anatole France, Edgar Allan Poe, Voltaire and Oscar Wilde.

Maurice Taquoy (1878–1952)

Horses and the racetrack were frequent subject matter for the painter and illustrator Maurice Taquoy, who was a lifelong fan of the races. Many of his fashion plates for *Journal des Dames et des Modes* and *Gazette du Bon Ton* depict the fashionable dress of women at such events. Taquoy also designed scarves for Hermès, which often uses equestrian motifs in reference to its origin as a purveyor of fine and custom-made saddles and tack.

Thayaht (1893–1959)

The Florentine artist known by the palindrome Thayaht was born Ernesto Michahelles. An accomplished painter, sculptor, engraver and goldsmith, Thayaht is best known for his association with the Italian Futurist movement, and less for his abiding interest in fashion and textiles. As part of a collaboration with Madeleine Vionnet in the early 1920s, Thayaht created original designs for the couturière and illustrated the Vionnet plates that appeared in *Gazette du Bon Ton*. In Italy, he worked on a wide variety of projects with the ultimate goal of inventing a new national style; he also wrote manifestos on the subject of fashion and supported a 'Made in Italy' fashion-design movement. His famous design for a unisex jumpsuit, which he called the *tuta*, is representative of the type of experimental clothing advocated by Futurist and Constructivist artists in the years immediately after World War I.

Armand Vallée (1884–1960)

In addition to his illustrations for *Journal des Dames et des Modes* and *Gazette du Bon Ton*, Armand Vallée was known for his risqué scenes featuring scantily clad girls, which he contributed to the humorous journals *Fantasio*, *La Vie Parisienne* and *Le Rire*. In common with many of his contemporaries, he also worked as a costume designer, most notably for the Paris Opéra. Vallée often found employment in the realm of advertising, illustrating posters and unique publicity products, such as a set of vintner's books on the history of French wine.

Gerda Wegener (1885–1940)

Gerda Wegener, who was born in Denmark, studied art at the Académie des Beaux-Arts in Copenhagen. In 1912 she moved to Paris with her husband, the painter Einar Wegener, who had been her teacher. Gerda found success almost immediately as an illustrator for magazines including *Journal des Dames et des Modes*, *La Baïonnette*, *La Guirlande* and *La Vie Parisienne*. She was also commissioned to paint many portraits and to illustrate numerous volumes of erotica, which are now highly sought-after by collectors of the genre. The Wegeners' marriage was annulled by the king of Denmark in 1930, after Einar became the first recorded recipient of gender-reassignment surgery, but the former spouses remained close. Gerda later remarried and lived in Morocco with her new husband before returning to Denmark, where she died in relative anonymity.

FURTHER READING

Babin, Gustave. 'Gravures de modes'. *L'Illustration*, 5 July 1912. Project Gutenberg, www.gutenberg.org/files/36357/36357-h/36357-h.htm (accessed 25 November 2014)

Bachollet, Raymond, Daniel Bordet, Anne-Claude Lelieur and Edmonde Charles-Roux. *Paul Iribe*. Paris, 1982

Barbier, George. *Pochoir: An Article from Arts et Metiers Graphiques Paris, 1937*. Pasadena, CA, 2000

Bass-Krueger, Maude. 'From the "*Union Parfaite*" to the "*Union Brisée*": The French Couture Industry and the Midinettes during the Great War', *Costume*, 47, no. 1 (2013), 28–44

Beach, Belle. 'Good Form on Horseback'. *Vogue*, 1 February 1922

Beaton, Cecil. *The Glass of Fashion*. London, 1954

'Beau Brummels of the Brush'. *Vogue*, 15 June 1914

Behling, Dorothy. 'French Couturiers and Artist-Illustrators: Fashion from 1900–1925'. Ph.D. diss., Ohio State University, 1977.

Blackman, Cally. *100 Years of Fashion Illustration*. London, 2007

Brainerd, Eleanor Hoyt. 'The Artist Dressmakers of Paris'. *Everybody's Magazine*, October 1905

Breward, Christopher, and Caroline Evans, eds. *Fashion and Modernity*. New York, 2005

'Cardinal Bans Tango'. *New York Times*, 10 January 1914

Chase, Edna Woolman, and Ilka Chase. *Always in Vogue*. New York, 1954

Curwen, Harold. *Processes of Graphic Reproduction in Printing*. London, 1963

Darrow, Margaret. *French Women and the First World War: War Stories of the Home Front*. New York, 2000

Davis, Mary E. *Classic Chic: Music, Fashion, and Modernism*. Berkeley, CA, 2006

Deslandres, Yvonne, Dorothée Lalanne and Didier Grumbach, trans. Paula Clifford. *Poiret: Paul Poiret 1879–1944*. New York, 1987

Doughty, Robin W. *Feather Fashions and Bird Preservation*. Berkeley and Los Angeles, CA, 1974

Downton, David. *Masters of Fashion Illustration*. London, 2010

Duff-Gordon, Lucile. *A Woman of Temperament*. Oxford, 2012; originally published as *Discretions and Indiscretions*. London, 1932

Evans, Caroline. *The Mechanical Smile: Modernism and the First Fashion Shows in France and America 1900–1929*. New Haven, CT, 2013

'Fashion: The Bakst-Paquin Combination'. *Vogue*, 15 June 1913

'Fashion: Fourrures Max'. *Vogue*, 15 March 1926

'Fashion: The House of Camille Roger'. *Vogue*, 15 April 1927

'Fashion: The House of Perugia'. *Vogue*, 15 June 1927

Fitzgerald, F. Scott. 'Echoes of the Jazz Age'. *Scribner's*, November 1931

Friend, Margaret Alice. 'An Interview with Monsieur Worth'. *Vogue*, 1 March 1912

——. 'Fashion: After the Manner of an Old Style-Book'. *Vogue*, 15 February 1913

Fry, Charles Rahn, and Carl Little. *Pochoir by Painters: An Exhibition of Books, Folios, Prints, and Ephemera, 1918–1938 From the Collection of Charles Rahn Fry*. New York, Metropolitan Museum of Art, [1988?]

Gascoigne, Bamber. *How to Identify Prints*. New York, 1986

Gerry, Vance. 'Pochoir: Practical Watercolor Stenciling of Illustrations & Designs for Books &c', in *Matrix 8: A Review for Printers and Bibliophiles*. Andoversford, Gloucestershire, 1988

——. *Pochoir: Practical Stenciling for the Modern Craftsman as Applied to Illustrations and Designs for Books &c*. Pasadena, CA, 1991

Harris, Elizabeth M. *Pochoir*. Washington, D.C., 1977

Holland, Vyvyan. *Hand Coloured Fashion Plates: 1170–1899*. London, 1988

Hollander, Anne. *Seeing Through Clothes*. New York, 1978

Ives, Colta Feller. *The Great Wave: The Influence of Japanese Woodcuts on French Prints*. New York, 1979

Kleinert, Annemarie. *Le Journal des Dames et des Modes: Ou la Conquête de l'Europe Féminine (1797–1839)*. Stuttgart, 2001

Koda, Harold, and Andrew Bolton. *Poiret*. New York, 2007

Lepape, Claude, and Thierry Defert, trans. Jane Brenton. *From the Ballets Russes to Vogue: The Art of Georges Lepape*. London, 1984

Mackrell, Alice. *An Illustrated History of Fashion: 500 Years of Fashion Illustration*. New York, 1997

——. *Art and Fashion*. London, 2005

McPhee, Constance C., and Nadine M. Orenstein. *Infinite Jest: Caricature and Satire from Leonardo to Levine*. New York, 2011

Martin, Richard, and Harold Koda. *Orientalism: Visions of the East in Western Dress*. New York, 1994

Martin, Richard Harrison. *Cubism and Fashion*. New York, 1998

Martorelli, Barbara. *George Barbier: The Birth of Art Deco*. Venice, 2009

——. *Gerda Wegener: La Vie Parisienne*. New York, 2009

Milbank, Caroline Rennolds. *Couture: The Great Designers*. New York, 1985

Paquin, Jeanne. 'Madame Paquin on "How I Create Fashions"'. *Vogue*, 1 November 1912

'Paris Holds Openings Despite War'. *New York Times*, 28 February 1915

Poiret, Paul. *Les Modèles de Paul Poiret: Printemps 1917*. New York, 1917

——, trans. Stephen Haden Guest. *My First Fifty Years*. London, 1931

——, trans. Stephen Haden Guest. *King of Fashion: The Autobiography of Paul Poiret*. London, 2009

Ray, Gordon N. *The Art Deco Book in France*. Charlottesville, VA, 2005

Reeder, Jan Glier. 'A Touch of Paquin, 1891–1920'. Master's thesis, Fashion Institute of Technology, New York, 1990

Ribeiro, Aileen. *Dress and Morality*. Oxford and New York, 2003

Ricci, Franco Maria. *Parisian Fashion from the Journal des Dames et des Modes*. New York, 1979

Saudé, Jean. *Traité d'enluminure d'art au pochoir*. Paris, 1925

Schleuning, Sarah, and Marianne Lamonaca. *Moderne: Fashioning the French Interior*. New York, 2008

SEM [George Goursat]. *Le Vrai et le Faux Chic*. Paris, 1914

Simon, Oliver. *Printer & Playground*. London, 1956

Steele, Valerie. *Paris Fashion: A Cultural History*. New York, 1988

——. *Women of Fashion: Twentieth Century Designers*. New York, 1991

——. *The Corset: A Cultural History*. New Haven, CT, 2003

Troy, Nancy. *Couture Culture: A Study in Modern Art and Fashion*. Cambridge, MA, 2003

Unno, Hiroshi. *George Barbier: Master of Art Deco*. Tokyo, 2011

Uzanne, Octave. *The Modern Parisienne*. New York, 1912

Vaudoyer, Jean-Louis, Henri de Régnier and Charles Martin. *George Barbier*. Paris, 1929

Ward, Gerald W. R., ed. *The Grove Encyclopedia of Materials and Techniques in Art*. New York, 2008

Weill, Alain. *Parisian Fashion: La Gazette du Bon Ton, 1912–1925*. Paris, 2000

'What Mrs Million Pays for her Hats'. *New York Times*, 17 July 1910

White, Palmer. *Poiret*. New York, 1973

Williams, Reba W. 'Pochoir Printing'. *American Artist*, 53 (1989), 70–75

Winterburn, Florence Hull, Jean-Philippe Worth and Paul Poiret. *Principles of Correct Dress*. New York and London, 1914

Zappia, Caterina. *Mostra di Enrico Sacchetti: Ritratti, Moda, Illustrazioni*. Legnano, Italy, 1989

ACKNOWLEDGMENTS

The authors are deeply grateful to the amazing staff and interns of the Special Collections & College Archives at the Fashion Institute of Technology in New York City. The holdings of this collection, without which the book would not have been possible, are the foundation of this publication. We are especially indebted to Karen Trivette, Head of Special Collections, whose support and encouragement have stewarded both authors beyond graduate school.

We would like to extend sincere thanks to Antoine Bucher and Nicolas Montagne, owners of Librairie Diktats in Lille, France, for their invaluable contribution of a rare item of ephemera and their expert knowledge on the use of pochoir in fashion illustration during the 1910s and 1920s.

Melissa Marra of The Museum at FIT generously shepherded image permissions of the Museum's holdings, while Carla Spencer and Edwina Tafoya of the Corrales Library in Corrales, New Mexico, supported research efforts throughout the project.

PICTURE CREDITS

INDEX

Page numbers in *italic* refer to illustrations

Adam, Paul 6
Aghion, Janine *206*
Antongini, Tom III–13
Art, Goût, Beauté 7, 16–17

Bakst, Léon 12, *13, 32*;
   Ballets Russes 54, *118,
   140*, 234; *Journal des Dames
   et des Modes 112, 118*
Barbier, George 7, *15,* 140,
   234, 235; *Gazette du Bon
   Ton 13, 139, 140, 148, 158,
   168, 178, 186*; *Journal des
   Dames et des Modes 112, 114,
   125, 135, 136*; *L'Eventail et la
   Fourrure chez Paquin 53,* 54,
   60–1; *Modes et Manières
   d'Aujourd'hui 76, 76, 85,
   88–95*
Beardsley, Aubrey 10, 20
Beaton, Cecil 12
Beer *174, 178, 180,* 232
Benito, Eduardo García *66,
   77,* 234; *La Dernière Lettre
   Persane 219–31*; *Gazette du
   Bon Ton 175, 180*; *Le Goût du
   Jour 205, 207*
Bernard, Tristan *98–9*
Bernouard, François 201,
   203
Besnard, Jean 140
Bianchini-Férier *183,* 232
Bobergh, Otto *144,* 234
Bok, Edward 15
Bonfils, Robert 234;
   Gazette du Bon Ton 180, 182;
   *Le Goût du Jour 202, 208,
   216*; *Modes et Manières
   d'Aujourd'hui 77, 102–5*
Boussingault, Jean-Louis
   166–7
Brissaud, Pierre 234–5;
   *Gazette du Bon Ton 9, 13, 139,
   140, 147, 152, 153, 157,
   170, 173, 174, 187, 203*;
   Le Goût du Jour 203, 216

Brock, Jan van *120, 122, 129*
Brunelleschi, Umberto 112,
   114, 142, 235

Callot Sœurs 14, *168,* 234
Carus, Arlette *134*
Cham (Charles Amédée de
   Noé) 189
Chanel, Gabriel 'Coco' 16,
   54, *180,* 235
Chaplin, Charlie *100*
Chase, Edna Woolman
   12–13
Cheriane, Mme Léon *217*
Chéruit 14, *139, 142, 152,
   157, 170,* 232
*Les Choses de Paul Poiret vues par
   Georges Lepape 35–51*
Corrard, Pierre 75–7
Les Créateurs de la Mode 54
Curwen, Harold 7

Dammy, Robert *130, 147,
   156, 165*
Daragnès, Jean-Gabriel *214*
Debucourt, Philibert-
   Louis *75,* III
Demay, Marcelle 12, *63–73,*
   139, 232, 235
La Dernière Lettre Persane 219–31
Deslys, Gaby *64,* 235
Diaghilev, Sergei 11, 140
Dœuillet *139, 146, 168, 174,
   187,* 232
Doucet *19, 139, 147, 154,
   155, 156, 157, 162, 165,*
   232
Doucet, Jacques 232, 236
Drésa, Jacques *154, 155,
   162, 202,* 235
Drian, Étienne 54, 112,
   121, 139, *171,* 235
Duchamp, Marcel 220
Dufy, Raoul 19, 20, *123,
   183,* 232

Eugénie, Empress *144,* 234
Everybody's Magazine 187

Fabius *137*
Femina 6, 11, 38, 76, III,
   220, 234, 235, 236
Femme 75, 76
Les Feuillets d'Art 16, 234
Fitzgerald, F. Scott *103,
   105*
Flores, Llano *204, 207,
   209, 212, 213, 215*
Fourrures Max 16, *219,
   220, 220,* 232–3
Franc-Nohain, Marie-
   Madeleine *116, 119, 120,*
   235
France, Anatole III, 236
Friend, Alice III

Gazette du Bon Ton 12, 12, 112,
   139–87, 201, 203;
   illustrators for *9, 13,* 220,
   232, 234, 235, 236;
   World War I 16, *94*
Gerry, Vance 7
Gorvel, Georges *211*
Gosé, Francisco Javier *143,
   146, 152, 162,* 235
Le Goût du Jour 16, 201–17,
   234, 235
Grangier, Jean *187*
Gris, Juan 220, 234
Grose, Francis 189
Guérin, Charles *210*

Harper's Bazaar 76, 234, 235
Honoré *122*
Hornaday, William T. 65

Les Idées Nouvelles de la Mode
   16–17
Illustrated London News 15
Iribe, Paul 20, *119,* 235;
   Gazette du Bon Ton 140;
   Knights of the Bracelet
   234, 235; *L'Eventail et la
   Fourrure chez Paquin 53,* 54,
   56–7; *Les Robes de Paul Poiret
   racontées par Paul Iribe 8, 10,
   10, 12, 19, 20, 20, 21–33,
   36,* 112, 189, 235

Jacomet, Daniel 7
Jenny 14, *168*
Joire, Henri *59*
Joire, Suzanne *59*
*Journal des Dames et des Modes 12,
   13,* III–37, *139,* 201;
   illustrators for 234, 235,
   236; as inspiration for *Le
   Goût du Jour 203*

Kunisada, Utagawa *10*

La Mésangère, Pierre de III
Lanvin, House of 14, *168,*
   233
Lanvin, Jeanne 14, 54, *173,
   174, 175, 211,* 233
Lanvin, Marie-Blanche *173,*
   233
Laurencin, Marie 20, *204*
Legrain, Pierre *123*
Leonardo da Vinci 189
Lepape, Georges 12, *12, 13,*
   64, *191,* 235; *Les Choses
   de Paul Poiret vues par Georges
   Lepape 35–6, 37–51, 75–6,*
   112, *221,* 235; *Gazette du
   Bon Ton 139, 140, 150, 159,
   172*; Knights of the
   Bracelet 234, 235;
   *L'Eventail et la Fourrure chez
   Paquin 53,* 54, *55*; *Modes
   et Manières d'Aujourd'hui 75–6,
   78–81, 96–7*
Leroy, Madame André *219,*
   232
Leroy, Maurice *183*
*L'Eventail et la Fourrure chez
   Paquin 53–61*
Lhuer, Victor *125, 133*
Loeze *118*
Louboutin, Christian 226
Louis XIV, King 15, 226,
   232
Louÿs, Pierre *60–1*
Lucile, Lady Duff-Gordon
   11, 54, *103, 135,* 233;
   hobble skirt *51, 126*;
   World War I 13, 15, 16

McClure 66
Martial et Armand 13, *168*
Martin, Charles 235;
Gazette du Bon Ton 13, *140,
149, 176*; *Journal des Dames et
des Modes* 112, 114, *120*;
Knights of the Bracelet
234, 235; *La Mode en mil
neuf cent douze chez Marcelle
Demay* 63, 64, 65, 67, 69,
71, 73; *Modes et Manières
d'Aujourd'hui* 76, 82–7;
Sports et Divertissements 85,
235
Martine 36, *39, 123*
Marty, André Édouard 7,
236; *Gazette du Bon Ton* 13,
140, *169, 177, 179*; *Modes
et Manières d'Aujourd'hui* 76,
98–101, 201
Matisse, Henri 7, 20
Méras, Paul *144*
Meynial, Jules 76
Michahelles, Ernesto *see*
Thayaht
Le Miroir des Modes 40
*La Mode en mil neuf cent douze chez
Marcelle Demay* 12, 63–73,
139, 232
Les Modes 11, *14*, 64, III
Modes et Manières d'Aujourd'hui
12, 16, 75–109, *139*, 201,
234, 235, 236
Modes et Manières du Jour 75,
77
Modigliani, Amedeo 20,
221
Monsieur 16
Montesquieu 219
Monvel, Bernard Boutet de
234, 235; *Gazette du Bon
Ton* 13, *140*; *Journal des
Dames et des Modes* 112, *124*
Mourgue, Pierre *184*
Muhammad XI *230*

Nast, Condé 16, *140*, 220
New York Times 14, 15, 54, 68,
71, 125, 129, 190, 201, *204*
*Nos Élégances et la Mode
Masculine* 64
Nos Étoiles 64, 232
Nozière 76

Paquin, House of 14, 53,
134, 139, *143, 148, 149,
158, 168*, 232, 233
Paquin, Isidore 53, 54, 59,
233
Paquin, Jeanne II, *11*, 15,
64, *134, 143*, 233;
Bakst-Paquin
Combination *118*;
*L'Eventail et la Fourrure chez
Paquin 12, 36, 53–61*, 112
Paquin & Joire 59
Perdriat, Hélène 204, *210,
236*
Perugia, André *187*, 233
Picasso, Pablo 7, 11, 20,
104, 220, 234
Pichon, Marcelle *181*, 203,
209, 215
Poiret, Denise *44, 129*
Poiret, House of 139
Poiret, Paul II, *12*, 15, 17,
54, 65, *129, 150, 159,
164, 165, 166–7, 177, 179,
183*; André Perugia *187*;
*Les Choses de Paul Poiret vues
par Georges Lepape 12, 13,
35–51, 75–6*, 112, 235; at
Doucet 232; and
Eduardo García Benito
220; hobble skirt *51,
126*, 190; Martine 36,
40, 123; Orientalism *12,
12*, 64, *160–1*, 233; *Les
Robes de Paul Poiret racontées
par Paul Iribe 7–8, 10–11,
10, 12*, 13, *19–33, 35, 36,
112*, 189, 233
Préjélan, Réné *184*
Prisca, Madame *184*, 234
Puget, Simon *164, 165*

Ray, Gordon N. 76
Redfern, House of 139,
152, 162, 163, 165, 168,
233
Redfern, John 233
Régnier, Henri de 76
Richepin, Jacques *12*
Le Rire 20, *119*, 235, 236
*Les Robes de Paul Poiret racontées
par Paul Iribe 19–33*
Robes et Femmes 189–99, 236
Rodier *183*

Roger, Camille *184*, 233–4
Romney, George 20
Rosette *58–9*
Rosine 36, *123*
Rzewuski, Alexander *179*

Sacchetti, Enrico 189–99,
236
Sachs, Hans 6
Satie, Erik 85, *104*, 140,
235
Saudé, Jean 7, *8, 9*
Schmid, M. 232
Schopper, Hartmann 6
Segonzac, André Dunoyer
de 20
Sellèque, Jean-Baptiste III
SEM 191, *191*
Sesboüé, Suzanne 114
Siméon, Fernand 77,
106–9, 114, *174, 183*, 236
Stefan, André *126*
Strimpl, Louis *151, 160–1,
163, 165*
Süe, Louis 36, *38, 39*

Talbot 66, 68, 70, 72
Taquoy, Maurice 236;
Gazette du Bon Ton 145, 157;
Le Goût du Jour 203, 207;
*Journal des Dames et des Modes
117*, 203
Le Témoin 20, 235
Thayaht 236; *Gazette du Bon
Ton 184, 185*
Toulouse-Lautrec, Henri
de 10, 20, *119*
Très Parisienne 16–17

Uzanne, Octave 63

Vallée, Armand *114, 115,
126, 127*, 236
Vanity Fair 220, 234, 236
Vaudoyer, Jean-Louis 54
Vernet, Carle and Horace
III
Vever *134*
Vionnet, House of 234
Vionnet, Madeleine II, 54,
184, 185, 232, 234, 236
Vogel, Lucien 139, 140,
201
Vogue 6, 10, 12, *14, 14*, 15,

16, 19, 20, 36, *59*, 64,
65, 76, *107*, III, *118, 124,
134*, 139, 140, *172, 180,
187*, 220, 234, 235;
Knights of the Bracelet
140, 234, 235, 236

Wanamaker, John 13, 63–4,
232
Wegener, Einar *131*, 236
Wegener, Gerda 112, *119,
131–3, 137*, 236
White, Palmer 220
Worth, Charles Frederick
144, 234
Worth, Gaston 190
Worth, House of 13, 19,
32, 54, 139, 144, *147, 157,
179, 185, 186*, 190, 232,
233, 234
Worth, Jean-Philippe 190

Zamacoïs, Miguel 219,
220, 221